1st U.S. Serial Rights

THEN GOD

By

Ivan Schoone

Scripture quotations are taken from the Revised Standard
Version of the Holy Bible, containing the Old and New
Testaments.

Old Testament, Copyright © 1952
New Testament, First Edition, Copyright © 1946
New Testament, Second Edition, Copyright © 1971
by
Division of Christian Education of the National Council of
Churches of Christ in the United States of America

Then God

Copyright © 2000 by Ivan Schoone

All rights reserved.

ISBN: 0-9678442-0-7

Library of Congress Catalog Card Number: 99-98147

Printed in the United States of America by Morris Publishing
3212 East Highway 30 • Kearney, Nebraska 68847 • 800-650-7888

ACKNOWLEDGEMENTS

To my wife, Patricia, who helped inspire this book and who edited and retyped much of this manuscript. My thanks go to Ruth Ann Nielsen who did considerable editing. To Melanie Thompson, who edited and retyped a substantial part of the manuscript. Without all of you, my family, I would never have completed this book.

CONTENTS

FOREWORD

When our Lord Jesus left this earth in a physical sense, He spoke to a group of twelve people, His disciples. Jesus gave them, as He has given to us through the Scriptures, the Great Commission in Matthew 28: 18 – 20.

In the King James Version of the Holy Bible, which I incidentally feel is most beautiful, He begins His final words by saying, *"All **power** is given unto me in heaven and in earth. Go ye therefore, and teach all nations, baptizing them in the name of the Father, and of the Son, and of the Holy Ghost. Teaching them to **observe** all things whatsoever I have commanded you. And lo, I am with you always, even unto the end of the world."* The words of Jesus!

These twelve men now had the task of spreading the gospel. I am certain they felt it would be the most difficult task anyone could possibly be commissioned for. They were told to "GO" and make disciples of all nations. They were told to "BAPTIZE" them in the name of the Father, Son and Holy Spirit, and then they were told to "TEACH" them to "OBSERVE" all things that He had commanded them. Last but not least, He gave them reassurance when He said, *"lo, I am with you always, even unto the end of the world."* Of over three hundred promises in the Bible this is the one that is probably relied on the most.

The purpose of this little book is to enlighten the reader. Within these pages you will "observe" the mighty "power" of the Lord God Almighty. Many religious individuals today have been taught that in order to enter the pearly gates, as many refer to Heaven, he or she "must" do this or that. They practice an "I must" religion. Often when that mission is felt accomplished, they indeed relax and say, "I did it!" I'm going to heaven," taking all the credit themselves. This kind of hypocrisy, I fear, will lead them in the exact opposite direction. Why? The Bible tells me so.

In the following pages, I will attempt to show that if anyone is going to be granted a golden seat in Heaven, it will be through the Almighty—the One Who has made and continues to make it all possible.

I ask you to be observant to what the Holy Bible tells us actually happened concerning God's plan of salvation. Even through sin, His plan was accomplished many times. Sometimes, it appears that if it had not been for sin, entire nations would have been lost. The lives of many individuals in Scripture would have gone by without any purpose.

The apostle Paul told the Romans in his letter, *"Where sin increased, grace abounded all the more"* (Romans 5:20). You will see in the coming chapters that sin was, indeed, on the increase. The Bible is full of illustrations of sin. At the same time, the love of God, His grace, certainly did abound and prevail in the lives of people the Bible teaches us about.

Did God cease to do His work or show His power when the last chapter of Revelations was written? I think not! The same God—the same yesterday, today and forever—is still at work in our lives as He was in men and women in the Bible. Just because there is not a Bible story exactly like our situation does not mean God is unreal. He is alive and well and continues to work in us and through us "His wonders to perform," as the saying goes. We just need to observe the power of God.

WHY SIN?

The origin of sin, as with many things in Scripture, is not perfectly clear. The Apostle Paul calls it *"the mystery of iniquity"* in II Thessalonians 2:7. Our finite minds are not a match for the infinite mind of God.

In reading through Scripture we get a glimpse of what might have happened either in the beginning, or perhaps prior to the beginning, of creation as we know it. Numerous Books of the Bible make reference to it.

It would appear, most theologians agree, that at one time there was a rebellion in Heaven. Lucifer, now referred to as Satan, was a mighty prince who thought he could be God. Subsequently, he was thrown out of Heaven, literally, and landed on this earth.

We find him first in the form of a serpent, a beautiful one at that, in the Garden of Eden. He was certainly attractive enough to beguile Eve.

The creation was over. God had everything in order. With His mighty fingertips, He placed the stars in the heavens, made the earth below, and, as the Bible says, "it was good." Adam was in charge of it all. However, Adam was lonely, so God decided he should have a helpmate, or a wife. Out of Adam's rib bones, God formed a fine woman whom Adam named Eve.

In this most beautiful of gardens there had to be order established. Not only was God creator of all things, He established Himself as Ruler and Lawgiver. He also gave man the power of choice, of good and devil. One tree in the garden was called the "tree of knowledge, of good and evil." Adam and his

1

wife could eat from every tree in the garden except that one. Both God and Adam knew that he wouldn't need the tree because he had it all. Paradise! The command from God didn't concern Adam: he didn't need the tree.

But the serpent, Satan, had a chat with Eve. He gave her a sales pitch about the tree. "Eat of it, your eyes will be opened, you will be like God, knowing good and evil," the devil coaxed her.

Sin often works this way. It's attractive; it looks good; it appears as if it's something we must have. Eve believed the serpent, took a bite of the tree's fruit, offered Adam a bite, and the Bible says, "He did eat." Sin is an abuse of freedom. We, like Adam and Eve, have a choice.

Like most things we do in life, once it's done, we cannot undo it. Adam couldn't either. When confronted by God, Adam blamed Eve, but it was no one's fault but his own. Sin had to be paid for. Adam was not as fortunate as we are to have a Savior to suffer and die on a cross for the sins of the whole world. That would happen thousands of years later.

God was angry! He set a curse upon the couple, kicked them out of the paradise garden, and reminded them of the pain they would endure until they would one day return to the ground from whence they came. But because of Eve's sin, instead of being equal with man, as it was and should be in a perfect society, Adam would from that point on, rule her (Genesis 3:16). It appears that since she proved herself incapable of making good decisions, Adam would be in charge. Centuries later, we are still trying to bring equality back from Eden. Think about it!

Sin was here to stay. Men and women would have to pay the price, and that price is depicted throughout the Scripture.

Genesis 3:16 begins with God declaring damnation on this couple: first Eve, then Adam. Then John 3:16 states the way of salvation for everyone, *"For God so loved the world, that He gave His only begotten Son, that **whosoever** believes in Him should not perish, but have eternal life."* "Whosoever" believes, male or female, shall be saved. It's another promise. In Genesis, He promises us difficulties in life from the very beginning of humanity. Then in John, when His physical life is nearly over on this earth, Jesus Himself promises us the gift of eternal life, which He has made possible.

Where sin increased, His grace increased. What a marvelous, merciful God. No wonder we search the Scriptures to find out all we can about Him.

There is a story of a young man who during a flood was drifting down a river about to go under for the last time. From out of nowhere, a hand reached out, grabbed him, and pulled him to the river's bank. He was saved!

Unfortunately, in the fury of trying to save others that were also in the same predicament, the near-drowned man lost track of the person who pulled him out. He searched the countryside for weeks, which turned into months, which turned into years, looking for the person who saved him. He had never thanked him, and he wanted to. But the man was a stranger just passing through the area that day. No one knew who he was, and no one ever saw him again. He may have been a salesman, a tourist, anyone. No one knew. Or could he have been an

3

angel *"unawares"* as Hebrews 13:2 talks about? The thankful man may never know, but he learned to thank God for sending his personal, little savior who saved his physical body. He also came to realize God as his spiritual Savior.

The young man may never know who pulled him out of the muddy river—what kind of man he was; where he was from. But thanks to God, he can know the One who saved him from his sins. The One who can be closer to him than any person could ever be.

GOD CLEANS IT UP

After the mess that Adam and Eve made out of life, one of their sons, Seth, became the one who would eventually produce another savior of the then-known world.

He is often called one of the most outstanding descendants of Seth: his name was Noah. Bear in mind that it is now hundreds of years since the earth was new. People had multiplied by the multitudes. The Bible tells us they had forgotten God and were committing every sin know at the time. However, "Noah found favor in the eyes of God," the Bible declares. His great-grandfather was Enoch, whom the Bible says, "walked with God" and was one of few men in Scripture who did not die: *"God took him"* (Genesis 5:24).

The fact remained that the world was full of wickedness. God was sick of it—man was out of control. Destroying them all became God's plan: spare Noah and his family and kill the rest via a mighty flood. God said, *"I will blot out man whom I have created out of the ground, man and beast and creeping things and birds of the air, for I am sorry that I have made them!"* (Genesis 6:7) Pretty scary!

I have always loved this story of Noah. It shows how God uses people even though, in the beginning of the ordeal, they didn't necessarily relish the idea of having God use them. Can you imagine this? One day, God called down to Noah while Noah was working in the fields.

"NOAH! NOAH"

Noah looks up into the heavens wondering where the voice is coming from.

"Noah, build me an ark 450 feet long, 75 feet wide and 45 feet high. Pair up all the animals, all the birds and your family. You have one hundred years to do it in," God tells him.

Noah probably hit the panic button. "Lord, I'm a farmer, not a carpenter," he most likely argued.

The Lord didn't care. "I will show you how to build it."

Then there was peer pressure. Can you imagine, every day for over 100 years people would come past the site where Noah, his wife and their three sons and their wives were building an ark on dry land? Miles from water! Noah was persecuted to the utmost. The townsfolk poked fun at him every day, probably thinking he had lost his mind. But the Bible says that Noah preached repentance for those 100 years, and besides his own family, not a single person listened to his message. We are not even sure they believed what was taking place.

Then one day it began raining. It rained the second day. That was probably not that unusual, but it rained again on the third, fourth and every day for forty days. People came up to the door of the ark, pounding on it saying, "Noah, Noah, let us in. We believe you now!"

But it was too late. The door of the ark was shut, and it stayed closed until the time the flood was over.

Many sermons have been preached about this man, Noah. I have used him many times in my sermons. Preachers love to invite their audience to the fact that "the door of grace is now open for all to come in," unlike the door of the ark when "God shut the door." Don't wait until He shuts the door again.

Now we have seen where sin, more or less, took over when the earth was new. God couldn't tolerate it anymore, so He wiped out most of civilization with the flood. God promised to never destroy the world again by water. The rainbow renews His promise each time that we see it.

God let people choose and make a mess out of things. Now we will see in the following chapters what appears to be God using sin to accomplish His mighty works. "His wonders to perform."

I should like to remind you that I am not an expert in theology. By the way, none of Jesus' followers were, either. I am only one who has observed the actions of God through the Scripture, as well as in my fifty-some years of life. I am convinced that in some manner, shape or form, *We know that in everything God works for good with those who love Him, who are called according to His purpose* (Romans 8:28). God often turns the "bad" things in our lives into "good." He can do that! He's God!

THE RESTLESS YEARS

Many times I've heard someone say, "I wish the Lord would speak to me, with a voice!" What they want is a conversation with God like the people of old did, when a voice boomed down from the heavens and instructed them with what to do or gave them direction by means of prophecy.

Well, back in those days, when the Lord spoke, often with that "still small voice" the Bible talks about, people didn't always take it seriously. Some did, those with much faith.

After the flood, it didn't take long for sin to once again get started. It is written that Noah planted a vineyard, made some wine and got himself drunk. It has been said, with tongue in cheek, that Noah probably had good reason to "tie one on" after all he had been through. That probably wasn't the answer, but remember: he was human.

Seems that when he became totally wasted, he evidently took his clothes off and lay there naked. Noah had three sons who would be the founders of the new human race. One son, Ham, saw his father and his nakedness and told his two brothers, Shem and Japheth, who took a garment to their father, not looking at him, and covered him.

But Noah knew that Ham had seen his nakedness. When he woke up, he pronounced a curse on Ham's son, Canaan. Canaan would be a servant, or a slave to Shem and Japheth. Here was one of the first classic examples of how the Lord did not curse the sinner, Ham, but cursed Ham's son, Canaan. We will see much more of this in later chapters.

Shem and Japheth received a blessing. Noah gave God the glory for the act of the two brothers. Shem, no doubt the first born, out of respect for his father, helped cover up his father's sin. The blessing to Shem assured him that God would always be his Father and continue in his family. Japheth, another one of the elder sons (Genesis 10:21), would, along with his family, live in the tents of Shem and be blessed along with them. Japheth's descendants would one day lead to the salvation of the Gentiles. Shem's descendants would be Jewish. The blessing can be interpreted that Jews and Gentiles are to live under one roof, so to speak. That was the ideal plan originating in the time of Noah.

The question here is what would have happened throughout history if Noah had not sinned? Like so many instances in Scripture, which I will elaborate on, we need to ask ourselves, what would have happened in the course of history if sin would not have been committed? Perhaps the answer, like a songwriter once wrote, is "blowing in the wind."

As the family of Noah reproduced and multiplied as God planned, the sin of pride appears to be the next factor to change the course of history.

Everyone on the earth was speaking one language—they were one big, happy family. They got the idea to build a huge city with a tower built straight towards the heavens. They had the materials to build bricks and mortar. Nothing could stop them.

God could see what was in their hearts. They were building something "they" could look at with pride and say "we" did it—much like many people today. The sin of pride, the sense of accomplishment, to make a name for themselves, which often forgets God. The focus became changed. No longer was it upon God but upon a creation they had constructed.

It was admirable that the people all wanted to stay together, but the way they pursued the venture was not in God's plan. God chose a way to create mass confusion. He would confound their language so they couldn't understand each other. He did it.

People were running to and fro in utter chaos. Eventually they sorted their families out and took off in every direction. God's plan. They scattered to every end of the world to form separate nations, each with a language of their own.

Abraham, or Abram, as he was called at the beginning of his life, was a man who feared the Lord with respect and reverence. This man is known by most today as the founder of the Jewish race. A direct descendant of Shem, he prospered in a land God showed him. Along with it came a blessing that God would also bless any man who blessed Abram, but the hand of the Lord would curse any man who cursed him.

One day, Abram, seeing his wealth, along with what was owned by his nephew Lot, whose father had died, decided they should split up. Lot's father, Haran, was one of Abram's brothers. The two families possessed great herds of livestock. Herdsmen for the two parties began to have problems with the livestock and would frequently create strife, the Bible says. The land in the immediate vicinity could not provide for all of them.

Together they went looking for a better place to live. When they arrived at a place north of what is now Palestine, they stopped. Abram should have had first choice of all the land, but being the kind of person he was, he allowed Lot to choose first. Naturally, Lot, seeing the rich, more productive and well-watered plain of Jordan, chose it. Abram more or less stayed where he was. The Lord told Abram he would have it all around, as far as the eye could see.

Along with a wealthy, rich land usually comes much sin, or so it would seem. Such was the case in the plains of Jordan, which Lot chose. A wicked city was located in the vicinity, and the inhabitants were committing every sin imaginable. The name of the town was Sodom. The Bible says, *"they were great sinners against the Lord"* (Genesis 13:13).

Softened by easy living, the people of Sodom forgot how to fight. They were invaded by a neighboring king and overtaken, including Lot and his family.

Hearing the news, Abram quickly prepared his small army and set out to rescue his nephew and family. He succeeded. Though he could have taken the "spoils," the riches of the area, he chose not to. Although he was offered an abundance, he refused, accepting only food for his tiny army. The people were grateful.

Lot chose to go back and live in Sodom with his family. Abram returned to his land in the plain of Mamre.

Not long afterward, the Lord, seeing the grave sins of Sodom, decided to destroy it. Abram argued and pleaded Sodom's case.

"Supposing fifty righteous people could be found in the city, would the Lord destroy it?" Abram inquired of the Lord, knowing that Lot and his family were all there.

But even Abram must have had second thoughts as he bargained the deal down to if only ten righteous were found in the city, would the Lord still destroy it? He felt the righteous should not perish with the wicked. Finally, the Lord assured Abram that for the sake of only ten, He would not destroy the city.

The Lord, knowing that ten righteous men could not be found in Sodom, sent two angels to pay Lot a visit. The so-called "men" of Sodom, both young and old, spotted them going to Lot's house. They surrounded the dwelling and asked Lot to send the two out so they could have their way with them. Lot said boldly, "NO!" In order to protect the two strangers, who Lot knew were angels, he offered the men of Sodom two of his virgin daughters "who knew not a man." But the men of Sodom wanted the two strangers for their sexual pleasures.

They beat on the door to the point of breaking it in. Suddenly the beating stopped. Instead of cries of lust, there were now cries of fear. The men of Sodom had been stricken blind by the hand of God, and the two angels were safe.

The next morning, the angels beckoned Lot to take his family and flee from Sodom, as fire and brimstone would destroy it and another wicked, neighboring town, Gomorrah. God had finally had enough of them. Only Lot, his wife and two daughters could be convinced to leave. The angels escorted them out.

They had all been instructed not to look back. But Lot's wife, wanting to look back and view the destruction of the city where she had once been so happy, did so. She was instantly turned to a "pillar of salt."

Sin was to continue. Lot's two daughters became concerned that their father would not have any offspring for the continuance of his name. They plotted to get him drunk, have sex with him, become pregnant, and their task would be complete. They did so, and each daughter had a son. One was named Moab, who became the father of the Moabites. The other was named Ben-Ammi, who became the father of the warring Ammonites. The two tribes would cross paths throughout Biblical history.

It's interesting to note that Moab became an ancestor of Ruth, who became a descendant of David, who was an ancestor of Jesus Christ. Matthew 1:1 states, *"The book of genealogy of Jesus Christ, the son of David, the son of Abraham."*

There were fourteen generations from Abraham to Jesus. The sins that were committed along the way were atrocious, but God used them as a means to accomplish His mighty works.

Even Abram was told by God Himself that his descendants would be so numerous he couldn't even count them. "Like the stars in the heaven, like the sands on the seashore," so many would there be.

Now it was Abram's turn to begin to wonder. He was 100 years old, his wife, Sarai, was 90 and there were still no children. The days of childbearing, scientifically, should have been long past for her. But God had other plans. First, there was a test of faith.

Upon receiving the blessing given by God Almighty and the promise of having a son, who would be named Isaac, their names would also be changed. Abram would now be Abraham and Sarai would now be Sarah. When they were told the good news, they couldn't believe it. They both laughed.

When Abraham was informed, he thought first his descendants would come from Ishmael, a son he had by impregnating Sarah's maid, Hagar. God told him no.

When Sarah was informed, she couldn't understand how this could happen. First she laughed as most women her age would. God did not appreciate her laughter, which showed a doubt in her mind. He corrected her about the matter in Genesis, chapter 18.

They had a son and named him Isaac, as they had been instructed. Prophecies were being fulfilled. Abraham's descendants were beginning to take shape.

JACOB & ESAU

One of the boldest acts of deception took place with the two sons of Isaac, Jacob and Esau. Deception is sin, and once again, we will see how sin changed, or perhaps forced to come to pass, the course of history.

In those days, the eldest son was to have the greatest of his father's possessions. Jacob and Esau were twins. Esau was born first by probably seconds. Jacob, it is written, grabbed hold of his brother's ankle in the process of being born (Genesis 25:26).

Esau, when he was delivered, came out of his mother's womb red and quite hairy for a newborn baby. Jacob, on the other hand, was born quite opposite, being of fair complexion.

Rebekah, their mother, whom the Lord also spoke to, knew the two boys would be trouble. She noted that they constantly struggled while in her womb. The Lord explained with prophecy, *"Two nations are in your womb, and two peoples, born of you, shall be divided. The one shall be stronger than the other, the elder shall serve the younger"* (Genesis 25:23). There it is! Now let's see how this was accomplished.

Esau was a great hunter, always in the fields and woods hunting game. His father, Isaac, delighted in the savory meat. Jacob was a homebody and the favorite son of his mother, Rebekah. Jacob had always wished he had been born first so he would be entitled to the birthright. It meant nothing to Esau at the time.

One day when Esau came in from an unsuccessful hunt, he was famished. Jacob was making soup and offered a bowl to Esau in exchange for his birthright. The birthright meant that Esau would receive a double portion of the inheritance when his father died. He would also be head of the family with all its responsibilities, which carried with it priestly privileges and duties. But Esau, being very hungry, sold it to Jacob for a bowl of soup and went on his way. Jacob now had what he longed for.

As the years went by, Isaac became blind. Esau, though he had not married wisely by marrying a Hittite woman, had caused much grief for his parents. In spite of the fact that Esau was a rebel, Isaac knew he had the duty of giving him the blessing and birthright. He could see death was not far away. He was unaware of what had taken place earlier with the sale of it.

One day, he summoned Esau to go hunting and bring him his favorite dish, fresh from the field. Esau was eager to go. Isaac informed him that upon his return he would eat and give Esau the blessing.

Rebekah heard this and began to scheme a plan with Jacob. She would help Jacob disguise himself like Esau: fake hair, Esau's clothes and whatever else they could do to fool Isaac. She cooked a mess of goat meat hoping to make old Isaac think it was wild game. She wrapped goatskin, with the hair outwards, on Jacob's arms and body just in case old Isaac would want to feel to assure himself it was really Esau.

The plan worked pretty well. Isaac questioned it, however, wondering how Esau returned from the fields so fast. He felt Jacob's arms and hands. The smell of the fields on his clothes helped convince the old man. He didn't quite think the voice was that of

Esau, but trusting his family, he went ahead and gave the blessing to Jacob.

When Esau returned from his hunting trip, he hurried to prepare the meal for his father. He soon discovered Jacob had beaten him to it. He begged for a blessing, the words from his father, Isaac that would make him the one whom all nations would bow down to. But no, Isaac informed him that his blessing would be that he would have to live by the sword and serve his younger brother. Esau hated Jacob and wanted to kill him.

Rebekah, learning of the plot to kill her favorite son, again intervened. She sent Jacob away to his uncle, Laban, where he would be safe while his brother's anger was being pacified. It was during this time that Jacob learned patience.

Jacob went to work for Laban. Laban had two daughters, Leah, the oldest, and Rachel, the youngest. Jacob fell in love with Rachel and wanted to marry her, if he could get Laban's consent. Working for his uncle, wages were involved. When Laban and Jacob discussed Jacob's wages, Jacob told Laban that instead of receiving money, he would be willing to work seven years if he could have Rachel as his wife. Laban agreed.

When the time was served and the wedding was to take place, it was Laban who performed the deceit. Instead of bringing out Rachel for the wedding, he secretly brought out Leah. Dressed with a heavy veil, Jacob didn't know the difference. The darkness of the night also contributed to Jacob unknowingly sleeping with the wrong person.

At dawn, it didn't take Jacob long to figure out which of Laban's daughters he had married. He went to Laban.

"Why have you deceived me like this?" he asked.

Laban convinced him it was the custom of the country to marry the eldest daughter first. Jacob was sad. Laban was greedy and wanted some more cheap help. He told Jacob that if he still wanted Rachel, he could have her if he would give Laban another seven years of labor. Jacob felt she was worth it, so he agreed. He waited for his love for fourteen long years.

It is said that Laban cheated Jacob on numerous occasions. Jacob lived with it and towards the end, they came to an understanding. They departed company, and it is written that Jacob "went on his way and the angels of God met him."

The healing of the two brothers was now ready to take place. Jacob was still concerned. He had accumulated a great deal of possessions by now and thought he would try to ease his brother's anger with gifts of livestock. It wasn't necessary.

When they met, the two brothers embraced one another and wept. Jacob offered his gifts, but Esau turned them down, saying he had enough possessions of his own. Later, upon Jacob's insistence, Esau reluctantly accepted the gifts. The two reunited.

Jacob now appeared to be at peace. He and his wives had twelve sons. Rachel was considered barren for years. Eventually, she and Jacob had a son, Joseph, who was to become a little savior to the entire nation of Jacob, now called Israel. Joseph, another recipient of a most sinful act, would prove that God was with him.

JOSEPH

Jacob was particularly fond of his boy, Joseph, because he was Rachel's son. Joseph was a son given to him in his old age and that made Joseph very special to him. Joseph was a favorite son, and Jacob made it very obvious to the rest of the family. This was a grave mistake to the human eye but not to God. God was able to use this partiality in His divine plan.

The Bible tells us Jacob made a robe with sleeves for Joseph. This was an unusual robe, different from just a robe wrapped around oneself. It was unique. Joseph's brothers despised their half brother for being awarded this fine garment by their father. "They hated him," the Bible says.

To make matters worse, Joseph was also a dreamer. To top that, he seemed to be very arrogant, instilling upon his brothers that he was better than they were. Society today would not accept this reality any better now than it did then. No one likes what appears to be a person who thinks they are better than anyone else.

What happened is this: Joseph had a dream. He called his brothers around him to have them hear it. He told them that in his dream they were binding sheaves in the field. In those days, wheat, for example, was cut with a sickle, picked up by hand and tied in bundles or sheaves. His sheaf stood upright, he told them, while theirs bowed down to his.

His brothers quickly interpreted the dream. "Do you think you are going to reign over us and dominate us?" his brothers inquired. And they hated him all the more.

Joseph, as if to add insult to injury told them about another dream where the sun, moon and eleven stars bowed down to him, signifying his family would one day bow to him. The brothers went to Jacob. He no doubt wondered himself about Joseph's wild dreams, but the Bible says, Jacob "kept the saying in his mind" even though he would not discover their real meaning until around twenty years later when the dreams would come true.

The brothers, overcome with jealousy and hate, plotted to kill Joseph. Had it not been for Joseph's brother, Reuben, the rest of the brothers would have killed him for sure. While in the wilderness fields tending their flocks, Reuben suggested placing him in a dry pit for safekeeping. They took his robe and wondered what to do with him next.

A band of traveling traders, who would be considered today as traveling salesmen, bought and sold just about anything imaginable. They even bought slaves along their way. The brothers decided to sell their brother, Joseph, to the traveling traders. They could get rid of him and have money besides— what a deal. They discussed how they would explain it to their father. They decided to splatter some goat blood on Joseph's robe and to tell their father that a wild animal killed him and ate him—probably could have been lions in that part of the country. Jacob bought their story and went into a deep state of mourning because his favorite son was dead.

Meanwhile, Joseph was on his way to Egypt, and an officer of the Pharaoh, Potiphar, bought him. Joseph "found favor" in the home of Potiphar where he was put in charge of many important things. They trusted him and noted that the Lord was with him. Joseph was eventually entrusted and put in charge of everything that Potiphar had, was made overseer of his house, and it is written that Potiphar's house was blessed because of Joseph.

All good things often come to an end. Joseph had a problem. He was young and good looking. The sin, often referred to as "the lust of the eye, " struck Potiphar's wife. She apparently wanted him as a sexual playmate. She wanted to use him for her own pleasure. No doubt her husband was gone a lot on business trips, and her sexual urges fell upon Joseph.

Joseph, being a God-fearing man, asked her a very thought-provoking question; a question many should ask in this day and age when confronted with a similar situation. "How can I commit this great wickedness and sin against God?" he inquired of her. She didn't know what to say, but continued to tease him and invite him to "lie with her."

One day, after being rejected many times, she conjured up a plan. When Joseph went to leave her presence, she grabbed a piece of his clothes and called out to the guards that he had attempted to rape her. When Potiphar returned home, she told him the same story. Potiphar became very angry and disappointed in Joseph and had him thrown in to prison.

Even in prison, or even in another form of pit, one could say, the Lord was with Joseph. The prison keeper could see it. He put Joseph in charge of the King's prison and *whatever was done there, he, Joseph, was the doer of it*" the Bible says in Genesis 39:22.

Prison was where God wanted Joseph at this time. For some reason or another, the Pharaoh's chief butler and baker were also cast into prison.

They had dreams, strange ones, that no one could interpret. Joseph helped them.

The butler's dream went like this: There was a vine in front of him. On the vine were three branches; it budded and blossomed. The blossoms turned into grapes. He had the Pharaoh's cup in his hand, squeezed the juice from the grapes into the cup and gave it to the Pharaoh.

Joseph explained to the butler what it meant. In three days the Pharaoh would restore him into office as the chief butler once again. Simple as that, but Joseph asked him to put in a good word for him when the butler returned to his duties. The butler, forgetting about Joseph, did not.

The baker had a similar dream where he had three cake baskets on his head with assorted baked foods for the Pharaoh. Birds were eating out of the basket. Joseph did not have good news for the baker. He told him that in three days the Pharaoh would behead him and hang him from a tree where birds would peck the flesh from his bones.

Three days after Joseph's explanation for the baker, it was the Pharaoh's birthday. He held a party and did, indeed, restore the butler to his old position as chief butler. He hanged the baker just as Joseph had predicted.

Two years passed. One day the Pharaoh dreamed he was standing by the Nile River. He beheld seven fat cows, which came up out of the river and ate the rich grass on the edge. Soon, seven thin cows also appeared and ate up the seven fat cows.

The Pharaoh awoke and went back to sleep and dreamt again. This time, his dream appeared to be as ridiculous as the first. Seven lean ears of corn ate up seven fat ears of corn. The Pharaoh awoke again, troubled. He called in all his magicians and people of knowledge to try and tell him what the dreams meant. Finding no help, it was then the chief butler remembered Joseph. "Oh, yeah," he probably told the Pharaoh. "A couple of years ago when I was in prison with the baker, there was a Hebrew there who interpreted our dreams and whose predictions came true."

It didn't take the Pharaoh long to summon Joseph. He had Joseph shaved and cleaned up. Then the Pharaoh told Joseph his dreams. The Pharaoh explained to Joseph that he had heard that Joseph could help him with the dreams. Joseph was humble and gave the credit to God, Who interpreted dreams through him.

"The dreams are one," Joseph told him. "God has revealed to Pharaoh what He is about to do," explaining that the number "seven" meant years. "There will be seven years of plenty and seven years of famine." He advised Pharaoh to pick a wise man and put him in charge of the preparation for this fourteen-year event, which would soon begin. He advised him that one-fifth of all food raised in the next seven years would have to be stored and put in reserve for the seven years of famine that was to follow. If he would not, they would all die—no ifs, ands, or buts.

Finding such and individual did not take Pharaoh too long. Since Joseph came up with the warning, Pharaoh decided that he should be the one to carry out the plan. So Joseph was put in charge of the land of Egypt, second in command only to Pharaoh himself. He assured Joseph that no one in the land would do anything without the consent of Joseph. He was governor—he was in charge!

At this time, Joseph was thirty years old. The Pharaoh's dreams had come true just as Joseph had foretold. In the land of Egypt, plenty of food was available for both man and beast, thanks to Joseph.

In Joseph's homeland, Canaan, things were different. Famine had struck. Hearing of food in Egypt, Jacob summoned his sons to go and buy food from the Egyptians. People from all the surrounding lands had to come to buy food or face the alternative: to die.

Now it was time for the brothers of Joseph to realize the fulfillment of their dreams that had occurred around twenty years prior. They arrived in Egypt and indeed bowed down before Joseph. Joseph recognized them but treated them as strangers. He, through divine providence, knew what he had to do, but it would all happen in due time. Joseph could see that the Lord's plan was beginning to take shape.

Joseph toyed with them. He called them spies and told them to return to Canaan and bring their younger brother, Benjamin, back with them. They were to leave one brother in prison for security until they returned. He pretended not to trust them. It was Reuben who remembered first what they had done years ago to their brother, Joseph, and recognized this as punishment. He reminded his brothers of it. Talking amongst themselves, the brothers did not realize Joseph could understand their language, but Joseph heard it all. He had to leave the room in fear of his brothers seeing him weeping. When he returned, he told them to leave brother Simeon with him. They watched as he was bound and escorted to prison.

Joseph then gave instructions to his staff to secretly put all the money back into the bags of grain that the brothers would be taking back to Canaan. The staff was to also pack provisions for their journey.

On their way home, they discovered the money in each one of their sacks, and they trembled with fright, saying, "What is this that God has done to us?"

When they arrived at home, old Jacob became very upset. He reminded them that he had already lost Joseph, and now he feared for Simeon, too. The ruler of Egypt wanted Benjamin; it was almost too much for the old man. Reuben, again, spoke up, assuring his dad that he would let Jacob kill his own two sons if either Simeon or Benjamin were killed. Perhaps Reuben also had divine assurance that everything would be well with them.

The family put off going back to Egypt until the last moments when they were again about to starve. They knew they must return with Benjamin or Simeon would be killed. Jacob even doubled the money to buy food on this trip and conceded the fact that if he must lose more sons, he would just have to lose them. They had no choice.

The brothers had a surprise when they arrived where Joseph lived: he invited them to his house. Still feeling guilty about not paying for the last batch of food, they tried to explain to Joseph what had happened. Joseph made light of their fears and assured them that God must have put the treasures in their sacks. Joseph had a feast prepared for his brothers, and Simeon was to be brought out to eat with them as well. Joseph kept these plans secret.

At noon, the brothers were brought to the house of Joseph. Their feet were washed, and their donkeys fed. Joseph inquired about the state of health their father was in, all the while pretending not to know them. When he saw Benjamin, he acted like he didn't recognize him, though he did. Again, he had to leave the room to weep tears of joy that his family was going to be together. When he had controlled himself, he returned. The food was served. The brothers were seated according to their ages, and they were amazed. Benjamin was given five times the portion of food than the rest of the brothers, but they were happy and enjoyed themselves.

Joseph instructed his staff once again to fill the sacks with food prior to them returning home and requested that the money be placed back in their bags. In Benjamin's sack, Joseph's silver cup was to be placed. He instructed his officers to let them get out of the city a distance and then chase them down. The officers were to then accuse the brothers of stealing the silver cup and doing Joseph wrong. The brothers would all be returned back to the city. All was done as Joseph requested.

Again, his brothers bowed down to Joseph. This time it was his brother, Judah, who tried to make a defense. Not knowing what to say about the false accusations, they had no defense but to tell Joseph that he could have them as slaves. Joseph quickly told them that only the one with the silver cup would be his slave, and the rest could go home in peace.

Judah would not give up, knowing that if they returned without Benjamin, their father would surely die. He told Joseph that their father, would not be able to take losing the only full brother of the one they had gotten rid of years ago.

Joseph could not control himself any longer. Seeing the innocence of his brothers and their repentant hearts concerning what they had done to him when he was a youth, he said, "I am Joseph." His brothers could not answer him. They were shocked.

The brothers were now more afraid, knowing the power that Joseph had. He could kill them all with a word, but Joseph chose to comfort them. He assured them that they shouldn't feel guilty. "God sent me before you to preserve life," he told them.

Then the awesome reality of the focus of this book came out of the lips and heart of Joseph. His brothers had cast him into a pit, not knowing if he lived or died after that, and sold him, like a little Jesus, for some quick cash—20 shekels of silver. He was to become a savior of a nation, to preserve life for the Israelites during the seven years of famine.

"SO IT WAS NOT YOU THAT SENT ME HERE, BUT GOD!" Joseph proclaimed to his brothers. The sin they had committed would be turned into good, as the Apostle Paul would tell the Romans hundreds of years later. *"We know that in everything, God works for good with those who love Him, who are called according to His purpose"* (Romans 8:28).

When Jacob died, Joseph's brothers were reminded one more time that what they had done to Joseph was forgiven and essential. Joseph said in Genesis 50:20, *"As for you, you meant evil against me, but God meant it for good, to bring it about that many people should be kept alive, as they are today."* God keeps His promises! In spite of their sins, the brothers would survive.

All the family of Joseph was brought into Egypt to dwell in the land of Goshen where one day God would raise up a man named Moses to bring them back out of this land. A land that had once saved them, Egypt would one day attempt to eliminate the Israelites because they would have a Pharaoh who refused to recognize God as Lord!

MOSES

The Israelites grew in number and a new king of Egypt had a problem with that. He became afraid that their population would become a threat to his internal security. The Bible says that he decided to make slaves of them, reduce their numbers, and make their lives become bitter.

Once again, we will see "where sin abounds, grace much more abounds." To enslave people is a grave sin. Many people, though, who are not actually "slaves" are slaves to something or another which we will discuss in later chapters. Slavery in any form is a sin. Now we have the situation in Egypt where God's people - remember that, God's people - who are like you and I, are literally slaves in need of freedom.

Often in Scripture, we find that where sin takes place, or abounds, God much more abounds. Many so-called Christians are under the belief that sin is only of the devil. Although that may be true, it is also true that if there were no sin, there would be need for a Savior to work His ways and wonders.

When these "righteous individuals" see sin, they are quick to condemn the individual or individuals. Their tunnel vision fails to see the effects, perhaps years down the road, and the works of God's master plan.

As is noted in the lives of many individuals in Scripture, if it had not been for sin, we never would have heard of them, and the Bible would not be near as thick as it is now. We would have lost a lot of its inspiration had it not been that God allows sin to abound just to show us that He is in charge.

Moses is no exception. When he was only three months old, Moses' mother, Jochebed, had to hide him from a rule the new pharaoh had made: all the boy babies would be thrown into the Nile River and drowned. This was his decree.

Little Moses' loving mother wanted him to live. Perhaps she already knew that one day he would be great. So she made him a basket out of bulrushes, waterproofed it, placed baby Moses in it and sent the basket and baby down the river.

Pharaoh's daughter was bathing in the river when she and her attendants spotted the basket floating towards them. She opened it and found the little Hebrew boy. He was crying. She felt sorry for him even though she was well aware that her father wanted him dead.

Jochebed wanted to have a hand in Moses' destiny. She commissioned Moses' sister, Miriam, yet a young girl, to keep an eye on the basket. Miriam watched it as the Egyptian women marveled at her brother. Miriam quickly and innocently went to the women and asked if they needed a nurse for the baby to suckle.

"Yes," the daughter of Pharaoh quickly responded, "and I will pay her, too." Moses was once again in the loving arms of his mother, safe from the wrath of the evil decree. This princess knew that she would get her way with her father, and he would allow the child to live.

The princess named the boy, "Moses," because she drew him out of the water. He was reared in the Egyptian culture along with all its pomp and pageantry. He was brought up like a prince. He learned the arts and crafts of the Egyptians, who were, at the time, unsurpassed in civilization. They were a brilliant people, excelling in many things.

Moses learned the law, the arts and leadership. He had it all.

God had other plans for Moses. The Egyptians were training him for leadership, but God would use it against them. Moses never forgot his heritage. He remembered where he came from: a humble Hebrew, a slave.

One day, he went out to his people and observed their burdens. He noted an Egyptian beating on one of his fellow Hebrews. Moses killed him. Murder! He buried him in the sand hoping no one would find out about it, but he was wrong.

Another day, he tried to settle a dispute among a couple of Hebrews. They asked him, "Are you going to kill us as you did the Egyptian?" Moses became afraid. He knew his life would be in danger if the Pharaoh found out about the crime.

Moses fled for his life to the land of Midian. As the New Testament writer of the book of Hebrews declared, "Moses refused to be called the son of pharaoh's daughter!" He chose a life of humility and hard times.

Thirsty from his desert journey, he discovered a well and drank of it, unknowing that this stop would change his life. The well belonged to Jethro who had seven daughters. While the girls were tending their fathers' flock, a band of neighboring shepherds came to help themselves to the well, pushing the girls aside. Moses drove the greedy and selfish shepherds away.

The girls rushed Moses home to meet their father. No doubt, each girl had their eye on this newly found friend, their hero, who had driven away the shepherds. Moses was invited in graciously by

Jethro, served a meal and learned that Jethro was a priest of the Midianites.

Soon, Jethro gave Moses one of his daughters, Zipporah. They had a son, and they called him Gershom because, as Moses said, "I have been a sojourner in a foreign land."

For forty years, Moses lived in the land a happy man. He had family, friends and respect. But was he indeed happy? His memories of Egypt haunted him. His kinfolk were still serving under the whip of their taskmasters. "They cried for help and God heard their cries," the Bible says. Moses, yet unknowing would be used by God to be their deliverer.

While tending the flock of his father-in-law one day on the west side of the wilderness, he came to Horeb, the mountain of God. He noted a bush burning, but the fire was not consuming it. He moved in for a closer look.

A Voice, thundering from the mountain boomed down to Moses. "Moses, Moses, do not come near, put off your shoes from your feet, for the place you are standing is holy ground."

God introduced himself to Moses as the God of his father, and Abraham, Isaac and Jacob. Moses was afraid. The Voice continued telling Moses that He had heard the cry of the Hebrews, and He had chosen Moses to deliver them out of bondage.

Moses argued, "Who am I to bring them out?" God assured him that He would be with him.

Moses was still not secure in his new commission. "Who shall I say sent me?" he asked. God answered, "I am who I am" sent you," He declared. "I am sent you," He added. The God of their fathers. God assured Moses the Hebrews would understand. Moses was still looking for excuses, as many of us do when we feel a "calling" to serve Almighty God. He was concerned that the people would not believe him, so God showed him a few miracles to perform to make them believers.

Moses took his staff, threw it to the ground and it became a snake. Grabbing it by the tail, it became a staff again. God instructed Moses to put his hand to his bosom. When he did, his hand was leprous, as white as snow. When he put his hand back to his bosom and withdrew it, his hand was perfectly normal again. God assured him that if the people failed to believe those two signs he should put his staff in the water of the Nile River when he got there, and it would be turned to blood.

Moses, however, continued his argument with God. "I am slow of speech and of tongue," indicating that he may have been a poor conversationalist or perhaps had a speech impediment.

God once again assured the doubter that He would be with his mouth and provide his brother Aaron, in Egypt, to speak for him if it was needed. "You shall be to him as God!" the Almighty told Moses. Many more signs could be done with his rod, God also reminded him.

The once reluctant Moses bid his family farewell and left on his trek to Egypt. His task: to free the people of Israel from Egyptian bondage. This was an enormous job, but with God, nothing is impossible.

Upon arrival in Egypt, Moses took Aaron aside and briefed him as to what the Lord expected of the two. Aaron related it to the people, and they were glad the Lord had finally seen their affliction. They immediately bowed their heads and worshipped the Lord.

Then came the hard part of addressing the Pharaoh with their demand to let the Israelites go. God had told Moses that the Pharaoh's heart would be hardened to the truth. Why would he not be? He had thousands of slaves busy building him a city. How would the task be completed if they should leave?

To convince the Pharaoh that this command was of God and that he didn't have much choice in the matter wasn't easy. This Pharaoh, who did not know God, would have to learn the hard way. When God speaks, one had better listen or suffer the consequences.

The Pharaoh did not listen and made life harder for the Israelites. Moses had wanted them to take a few days off their labors and go to the wilderness and make sacrifices as the Lord had commanded. Pharaoh, out of meanness, told the slaves to continue making bricks. One of the main ingredients, straw, would be taken away. He took away the straw and commanded them to make the same number of bricks without it. They could go find some straw for themselves, but that would take too much time going to the fields and searching the stubble for what straw was left. As a result, the numbers of bricks made per day were not adequate, and the taskmasters beat the slaves.

When the Lord's commands are not met, there will be a price to pay. This was the case for Pharaoh. Moses used his rod to perform acts that should have changed the Pharaoh's mind. When Moses cast the rod on the ground and it became a serpent, the royal magicians could do the same thing, so the Pharaoh was not impressed with what Moses had done.

Moses touched his rod in the waters of the Nile River, and it turned to blood - undrinkable to man or beast. It became foul and putrid after the fish began dying. The Egyptians tried to find water elsewhere, but to no avail. After seven days, Moses approached the Pharaoh saying "let my people go," or else. The Pharaoh refused.

Frogs, frogs everywhere. Wherever you walked, sat or laid, there were frogs. The Pharaoh, for a moment, agreed to let the people go if Moses would get rid of the frogs. The Lord eliminated the frogs at Moses' request, but the Pharaoh again hardened his heart and went back on his word.

Then came the plagues of gnats and flies, so thick that the people of Egypt could not escape them. The Pharaoh again agreed to let the people go, and again lied.

The plague of the death of the Egyptian livestock would surely persuade Pharaoh to let God's people go. During this plague, the Israelites' livestock were not harmed and that bothered the Pharaoh. He could see God at work, but through his hardness of heart could not give in.

The Egyptians became plagued with boils and sores. Hail and fire consumed their homes, fields and flocks. Locusts came and cleaned up what the hail didn't get. Darkness filled the land of Egypt for three days. It was black as pitch. The heart of the Pharaoh was beginning to soften, or so it appeared. One more plague would be needed.

The proverbial "straw that broke the camel's back" came when the Lord would kill all the first born of Egypt. The Israelites could escape this plague by wiping blood on their doorposts to alert the angel of death that their house was to be passed over. This was the institution of the first Passover, a day that is still remembered and celebrated to this day.

Pharaoh had to crack under the strain of death. His son died along with all the first born of Egypt. He wanted the Israelites out, the quicker the better. He had finally had enough!

When the people were nearly free, the Pharaoh again had a change of heart. He took his army and pursued them, intending to bring them back. When a pillar of fire obstructed their path, he had to stop his chariots.

The Israelites had a problem, too. The Red Sea was in their way to freedom. With Moses as their leader they had nothing to fear. He stretched out his rod, given to him by God Himself, over the water. The Red Sea parted, allowing His people to cross the sea on dry land.

The pillar of fire that had stopped the Egyptian army also died out, and they moved forward in pursuit. With the Israelite nation safely across, the waters closed back to normal, consuming the pursuing army of Egypt. God's people were free at last.

The people of Israel were not without fault. They would grumble at the least little problem. With a lack of food and water, some felt they were better off back in Egypt. The Lord supplied them with everything. Bread rained down from heaven. Water came bubbling out from a rock where, scientifically, no water should have even been. God took care of them in spite of their unbelief and lack of faith.

The Lord God gave them a book of laws made "with the fingertip of God." The book was given directly to Moses, a one-time murderer, who became the lawgiver of an entire nation as well as future nations. Moses, a sinner, became the lawgiver of not only the ten commandments, but also laws pertaining to everything imaginable—from how one should always conduct themselves to the high judicial laws of the land. God gave them all to Moses.

When Moses was 120 years old, it was time for him to die. God took him to Mount Nebo. The Bible says that God buried him. To this day, no one knows where. It was said of Moses that "his eye was not dim, nor was his natural force abated." God kept him young.

There has never risen a prophet out of Israel like Moses who knew the Lord "face to face." No one else performed as many signs and wonders as he did. Because he sinned, God would not allow him to set foot on the land He had promised to Abraham, Isaac and Jacob. However, He let him see it in all its beauty. Moses will always be remembered as a true servant of God working hand in hand with the Almighty, His wonders to perform.

Moses was a man so important to God that he was present at the Mount of Transfiguration where he, along with Elijah, talked with Jesus (Matthew 17:1-13).

RAHAB

Prior to the death of Moses, another great man named Joshua was commissioned by the great prophet to lead Israel across the Jordan river to the promised land. The Lord spoke to him as He had Moses. Everything God had promised to Moses would now be fulfilled to this mighty military man who was skilled in conquering the enemy.

Knowing that the Lord would be with him in all his undertakings, Joshua set out to do as the Lord had commissioned him. Commanded by the Lord to *"be strong and of good courage,"* (Joshua 1:9), Joshua couldn't lose. By using his God-given talent as a military man, and with God's help, he had it made.

He made a few mistakes, as all humans do, but he prevailed. He blundered the treaty with the Gibeonites. He also failed in not occupying the fortress of the Jebusites. Joshua became, to some degree, isolated from the northern tribes. Though his campaigns had broken the power of the Canaanites, he had not exterminated them. The prospect of further fighting with certain tribes remained.

A very noteworthy individual in the book of Joshua is a lady by the name of Rahab. The Bible tells us she was a harlot, or prostitute. So here we will see once again how God uses what is often considered by some to be the worst of people to accomplish His ways.

Joshua was about to conquer Jericho. Not knowing how fortified it was, he sent spies into the city to check it out. Somehow, word had leaked out that Israel was going to do this very thing. The king of Jericho learned that the spies were staying at the boarding house run by Rahab, so the king sent some of his soldiers to search out the spies. Rahab saw them coming. To the amazement of Joshua's spies, Rahab quickly hid the men on the roof of her home by covering them with the flax stalks she had on the roof to dry. The men were safe. Rahab sent the king's men on a wild goose chase to the Jordan River where she informed them the spies had gone.

Despite the kind of woman she was, Rahab respected and feared the Lord. She had heard the stories about Moses crossing the Red Sea and countless other stories of the great miracles the Lord had rained on the people of Israel. Now, some of the men who knew the Lord well were in her house and about to bring terror upon the town where she and her family lived.

It was time for her to make a deal. She told the spies that because she had hidden them, they should spare her and her family. When they came to destroy the city and all it's inhabitants, she wanted herself, her parents, brothers, sisters, and everyone who was considered close to them, spared. The spies agreed, "our life for yours." She had to promise not to tell anyone about the fact that they had been there. She agreed. To secure the plan, the spies told her that when she saw the army coming into town, she should hang a scarlet cord out the window of her house and have all her family inside it, and they would not be harmed. She agreed.

Rahab watched the spies sneak out of town. When they returned to Joshua, they assured him that the entire town was scared to death of them. The townspeople, like Rahab, were familiar with the Israelite success stories they had heard concerning the Lord being on their side. They were all aware that they would be no match for an army, which had the Lord God Almighty fighting with them. They were afraid. Joshua, knowing that fear was to his advantage, proceeded to make plans for conquering Jericho.

Joshua led his 40,000 troops towards the Jordan River to prepare to cross over onto the plains of Jericho. As the Lord had done for Moses at the crossing of the Red Sea, he did again for Joshua at the Jordan. The river was mighty at that particular time of year; overflowing its banks. It would have been difficult for his army to cross, but God made it possible. "With the breath of his nostrils," as Moses said, he parted the waters so everyone could cross on dry land.

A memorial was built using twelve stones, one for each tribe of Israel, commemorating the miracle. God exalted Joshua, like Moses, to the people. They stood in awe as the waters parted, and Joshua deemed it necessary to give God the glory by building the memorial.

For seven days, Joshua's army marched around the fortified walls of Jericho. The walls were thick stone and next to impossible to penetrate. Joshua had a plan, and on his command, it was implemented. At his order, the trumpets sounded and the people shouted. The noise was enough to make the great wall tremble and shake and fall flat to the ground, making it possible for his army to walk over them.

Joshua reminded the army to be aware of the scarlet cord at the house of Rahab. The two spies whom she had protected went to her house and rescued Rahab and her family as they had promised. Everyone else in the city, young and old, including livestock, were destroyed "by the edge of the sword," it is written.

Rahab and her family lived in the land of Israel the rest of their days because she had hidden the messengers, the spies, of Joshua. A prostitute became a little savior of not only Joshua's men but her family as well. God used her in spite of herself to fulfill His purpose.

Today, we often look down upon those who, like Martin Luther said, "sin boldly." Their sin is obvious, but God can turn that around to His benefit and most importantly, to the benefit of the individual. Pious Christians often fail to be able to relate to this fact of Scripture, thinking God only uses those who do His will and practice His teachings.

One never knows what day, what hour, God will touch the life of a bold sinner as He did Rahab and has done to so many others. Perhaps God does it to confuse the self-righteous as the Bible talks about in I Corinthians 1:20-31. We can never dare to speculate when it comes to God and His infinite wisdom. Once again, He proves His infinite mind is not a match for our finite minds. He's God!

Rahab, it is written, became the wife of Salmon and the mother of Boaz, thus becoming a direct descendant in David's line of our Lord Jesus (Matthew 1:5). A prostitute is an ancestor of Jesus. How about that! There's hope!

GIDEON

With Joshua long gone and Israel at peace, the people became content. Too content! They prospered, married into heathen tribes and thought they would never have to fight a war again. They had forgotten the goodness of God. All the profound deeds of men like Moses who led them out of Egyptian bondage were soon forgotten. They now even worshipped the false gods of Baal and Ashtoreth, and the Lord God was unhappy with them.

As it is written, and historically true, whenever people get too content and appear to be happy in their sins, God has a way of getting their attention. There is a saying, which states, "God whispers to us in our happiness, but He shouts at us in our pain." Such was the case of the children of Israel. God needed to get His chosen people back on track.

Israel had many enemies. Tribes with huge numbers were conspiring to take over, and Israel was asleep. To make matters worse, they had alienated God with their idol worship, and God had enough. It was time for the awakening, a lesson they would never forget. For the next seven years, the Israelites would be delivered into the hands of their enemies, the Midianites and their allies, the Amalekites. Their enemies would literally plunder, pillage and rape the land and the people. God began to shout at them through their pain!

Out of this chaos arose a man of God named Gideon. God referred to him as "Oh mighty man of valor." He refused to believe that the Lord was not concerned about them but at the same time wondered, "Why then has all this befallen us?" he questioned God's messenger. The Lord turned to him and informed him that he, Gideon, was to be the deliverer of the nation of Israel.

Like Moses, he argued to some extent with the Lord. Since his clan was the weakest of all the Israelites, he wondered how could he save anything? Then the Lord had to remind him, "I will be with you and you shall smite the Midianites as one man." Wow!

Gideon destroyed the altar of Baal, the first thing on his agenda. He did it at night so no one would know who did it. He was fearful of the consequences. But the people soon figured it out. They went to Joash, Gideon's father. He took the side of his son, although he, himself, had contributed to the building of the false god. He told the people that if Baal was not happy with Gideon, let Baal punish him. After they thought about it, their imaginary god couldn't do anything, and they turned their respect back toward Gideon.

The Midianites and the people of the East were about to swarm the Israelites camped not far away. Gideon summoned his allies, which soon numbered around 32,000 men.

Gideon still had doubts, and he tested his Lord by asking for a sign assuring him his army would prevail over the enemy. He laid out a fleece of wool one night on the threshing floor and proceeded to make a deal with the Lord, stating that if the fleece had dew on it and the floor was dry, then he would know that the Lord would deliver the Israelites from their enemies. The next morning the fleece had enough dew on it to fill a bowl, and the floor was dry.

Now Gideon still had doubts, and he talked with the Lord a second time saying he didn't want to make Him mad, but could he test Him again? If he laid the fleece out on the floor and the next morning the ground was wet with dew and the fleece was dry, then he would be certain the Lord meant what He said. The Lord went along with the plan, and sure enough, the next morning, the fleece was dry and the ground was covered with dew.

Gideon was satisfied and had even tested the Lord and gotten away with it. This act is not advisable for the modern day individual because it expresses our lack of faith.

Gideon was ready for war. His troops were ready and the Lord spoke to him again. "You've got too many soldiers," He told Gideon, who no doubt wondered if he had enough. But Gideon listened to his Lord.

After asking those who were afraid to fight to leave, he still had 10,000 men left. The Lord told him he still had too many.

The Lord told Gideon to take the men to the river to get themselves a drink. Whoever scooped up water with their hands and brought it to their mouth with their eyes watchful, much like a wild animal would do, lapping water with their eyes searching for danger, would be his army.

When the test was complete, Gideon had 300 men left. The Lord said it was all he needed to win the war.

With the handful of soldiers, the Lord laid out His plan to Gideon: give them each a big jar with a lit torch inside; in the other hand, give them a trumpet. Armed with these weapons, they were to surround the Midian camp in the middle of the night. At the command, they would blow their trumpets, break their jars so the torch was exposed, and shout, "For the Lord and for Gideon!"

Gideon's army did as they were instructed. The enemy army, startled at the noise and lights surrounding them, thought they were outnumbered. In the darkness and ensuing confusion, they began fighting and killing their fellow soldiers. Those left alive scattered to the hills and left the country in fear of their lives. Gideon, with the help of his Supreme Commander and Chief, won the battle.

Gideon, being human, made a mistake, though. While he is depicted as a very faithful and God-fearing individual, the Bible tells us he, too, may have fallen somewhat. From the spoils of his enemy, he had an ephod made as sort of a memorial to the victory over the Midianites and their allies. He had the object made from gold, jewels and fine things worn by the kings of Midian. He had the ephod on display in his city called Ophrah. The Bible says in Judges 8:27, "...all Israel played the harlot after it there, and it became a snare to Gideon and his family." It's dangerous to mess with idol worship.

According to theologians, the ephod became more important to the people than an altar already built by divine command. By reducing the importance of God's altar, it "became a snare to Gideon and his family." It is believed that the act concerning the ephod ruined the family of Gideon.

As the years went on, Gideon died, and it didn't take long for the people to forget Gideon and his greatness. The Israelites once again began the worship of idols.

SAMSON

Because they alienated God, worshipped idols and lived in sin, Israel was under the control of the Philistines for around forty years. During this time an angel of the Lord appeared to a man named Manoah and his wife. The angel informed the couple they would be having a son. It was a shock to them, as the wife of Manoah was barren, much like Sarah, Abraham's wife, was. Once again, we will note that with God, nothing is impossible.

Along with the word that she would conceive were certain conditions. The son would be a Nazarite and would be subject to Nazarite laws, but not necessarily fall under them. The angel told his mother that she should not consume any wine or strong drink or eat anything unclean while the baby was either in her womb or suckling at her breast. Finally no razor should ever touch his head.

Living with his parents in Dan, which was an area next to the land of the Philistines, the lad grew up to be very strong and handsome. "The spirit of the Lord was with him!" is the statement the Bible refers to in reference to Samson. He was to be another deliverer of the fallen Israelites. He was a judge over the land and was respected by his followers and enemies as well.

But the young man is also referred to by scholars as being very strong but weak in character. Samson had a problem with passion towards the women. He was also a tease and loved to intimidate people, especially his enemies. Yet God had use for this flaunting individual.

One day, Samson visited a town called Timnah where he spotted one of the daughters of the

46

Philistines. He wanted her and wanted her that instant. He returned home and more or less ordered his parents to "get her for me, she pleases me well." He wanted her for his wife.

His parents were not happy with his choice, arguing with him to pick a wife out of his tribe and not from the heathen Philistine neighbors. Samson was strong-willed and insisted on having this gal he had his eye one. His parents did not know that what their son wanted was actually a message from the Lord. What better opportunity to confront the Philistines than to go after one of their women?

Samson headed toward the town where he had seen her. On the way, a lion got in his way, and he killed it with his bare hands. He continued on his way and picked the lady up. They talked of his dreams; then he returned to his home. Samson decided he wouldn't tell his parents of the fight with the lion.

On his way home, he happened to pass by the dead carcass of the lion he had killed. Samson noted a swarm of bees had built a hive in the carcass. He scooped up the honey, ate some and then took some with him and shared it with his parents.

It was time to party, as was the custom then, as we do when a couple gets married. Perhaps a bachelor party was held while his father went to get the woman he loved. Thirty of Samson's companions attended. Samson had a riddle for them. He made a deal with them, sort of a bet that they couldn't figure out his riddle. If they could not, they would have to give him thirty linen garments and thirty festal garments; an expensive array of clothing. They would have seven days to come up with the answer. Here's the riddle: *"Out of the eater came something to*

47

eat. Out of the strong came something sweet" (Judges 14:14). What is it?

If they would guess the answer, Samson would give them the garments, but if they could not, they would have to give them to him. The thirty friends had a problem: they could not figure out the riddle. They approached his wife to try and convince her to get it out of him. "Entice your husband," they begged her. They threatened her to the point of murder if she would not. She did as she was asked, telling Samson if he couldn't share his secret with her, it was because he didn't love her enough to share it. She cried like a baby.

On the seventh day of the feast, he finally told her. She went directly to the men and informed them of the riddle's answer. They, in turn, couldn't tell Samson fast enough. Now they wouldn't have to pay for the garments in the deal. "What is sweeter than honey and what is stronger than a lion," they told Samson.

Samson's anger was kindled. He knew how they found out and told them so. "If you had not plowed with my heifer, you would not have found out my riddle." He went to the next town and slaughtered thirty of their countrymen for revenge. He took their garments and festal wear and paid off the debt he owed to the men. He went to his father's house and told his father about the ordeal. His father, in turn, gave Samson's wife to the man who had been Samson's best man in his wedding.

After awhile, when Samson's temper cooled, he went home again to his father's house. He thought he would have relations with his wife who, unknowingly to him, was married to another by now. When he found out the news, Samson had another excuse to get at the Philistines. He caught and bound three hundred foxes, tail to tail, put a torch between each pair of tails and let them loose across a big wheat field belonging to the Philistines. The wheat was dry and ready for harvest. Tinder. The olive orchards went up in smoke, too. The Philistines were mad and soon learned who was responsible.

To get even, the Philistines conducted a raid on one of the Israelite towns. Three thousand Israelites went to Samson and wished to bind him and deliver him to the Philistines. Samson let them, as long as they did not kill him. They agreed. So with two new ropes, they tied him, arms and hands, and turned him over to the Philistines.

Thinking he was secure, the Philistines had no idea what was about to take place. Once again, "the Spirit of the Lord came mightily upon him" and Samson broke his ropes, picked up a fresh jaw bone of an ass or donkey, and killed around a thousand Philistines.

Once, while in the wilderness, Samson was thirsty. As the Lord had done with so many people, he provided water for the mighty Samson and delivered him from death by thirst. He went on to judge Israel for twenty years.

During his travels, his objective was, and always had been, to see how many Philistines he could slay, or so it seemed. This mighty man, God's appointed for the task, slept with prostitutes and delighted in beautiful women. Yet he was God's man.

He did manage to fall in love again, but it was with another Philistine woman by the name of Delilah. The lords of the Philistines approached her to find out the secret to his strength. They would pay her well.

She tried, but only to fail as each time Samson would lie to her and would then have the opportunity to kill more Philistines. One time he told her that if he was tied up with seven fresh bowstrings, "I will be as weak as any man." Other times he would tell her that to tie him with new ropes or to tie his hair into seven locks woven into a web would make him weak. But it was all a mockery for Delilah. Each time, she would have men waiting to kill him. Each time, Samson and his strength became the executioner.

But then like his first love had told him, Delilah found the perfect line. "If you loved me, you would tell me the truth." Samson weakened and told her his secret. Shaving his head would indeed make him as weak as any man. While he slept, she did it - cut off all his hair. She called the Philistines, and they subdued him. The vow Samson had with God concerning his long, flowing hair was broken, and like most vows broken with God, Samson became weakened.

The Philistines not only captured this great hero of the Israelites but chose to make sport with him. They gorged out his eyes and made him grind flour at the mill doing the work of a horse, turning the mill stone one revolution after another, day after day.

One day, the Philistines decided to make a tribute to their god, Dagon, a fish-like idol. In their drunken party spirit, they thought it would be fun to call on Samson to entertain them. They sent for him in his prison cell. A young lad was chosen to place him between two pillars that held up the roof of this gymnasium-type structure. Around three thousand people were on the roof alone, while probably thousands more were in the building.

What the Philistines forgot was that while they had Samson in prison, his hair was growing back. His strength was returning. His power indeed was returned when he looked up into the heavens and asked God to "just this once" give him the strength back to avenge his captors. He would die with them; that was fine with Samson.

When the Spirit once again filled Samson, he, with a mighty shove and mighty pull moved the pillars which supported the building. Much like dominoes, move one and the rest crumple, it all came tumbling down. He ended up slaying more Philistines in his death than he had during his life, the Bible says. The Lord once again, through Samson, defeated the enemy.

Like so many individuals in Scripture, a sinful man became God's instrument to accomplish His mighty acts. If Samson were among us today, no one would ever believe he would be chosen by God to do His work. A man who sleeps with prostitutes, disobeys his parents and does as he pleases surely is not a God-fearing man. Or is he?

RUTH

From a mountain peak in the land of Moab, Moses was allowed to view the promised land years ago. During the time of Ruth, the Moabites worshipped all sorts of strange gods and were looked down upon by most Israelites. If you were from Moab, you were nothing to most and possibly heathen.

Yet, it was fairly common for people to move from the land of Israel to a country like Moab. There was peace in the land, and life was fairly good. One could prosper, and no one needed to go hungry.

Because there was a famine in the land of Israel, a man by the name of Elimelech, his wife Naomi and their two sons, Mahlon and Chilon, left the land of Israel. They chose to dwell in Moab where the pastures were green and prosperity was possible.

Elimelech died leaving his widow and two sons who would care for her. They each chose a wife, which was a comfort to Naomi. The more help she had, the better. She had good relationships with her daughters–in–law.

Unfortunately, luck was not Naomi's fate. She was depressed. Although it is not known how it occurred, her two sons also died. In a matter of ten years, daughters-in-law Ruth and Orpah were also without husbands.

Naomi made the decision to travel back to her native land, Israel. She had heard the famine was over, and she was more comfortable among old family members and friends. Ruth and Orpah were obligated, and they wanted to go with her. Naomi thought about it and evidently felt that Ruth and Orpah should stay with their families in their own land. After some debate, Orpah decided to stay in Moab, but Ruth insisted upon clinging to her mother-in-law, travelling with her and caring for her. It was at this point when Ruth made the famous statement to Naomi, *"Entreat me not to leave you or to return from following you, for where you lodge I will lodge, your people shall be my people and your God, my God"* (Ruth 1:16). Seeing Ruth's determination, Naomi agreed.

They ended their journey in Bethlehem, which as you will see later, is quite ironic. After settling in, the next priority was to earn a living or find food. Because harvest was in full swing, small grains were being harvested. Poor people were allowed to glean the fields after the harvesters shocked the grain.

Naomi had a relative, or kinsman as they were called, that owned land. His name was Boaz. Naomi knew that Ruth would find favor with him, and he would allow her to glean his fields.

After introductions were made, Boaz was more than happy to let Ruth glean. He even instructed her to glean behind his women in the fields and assured her that no man would try to molest her. She was a beautiful woman and it would not be uncommon that men would take advantage of a lone woman in the fields.

Ruth continued to glean in the fields of Boaz. One night while Boaz lay sleeping on the floor where the threshing of barley was being done, Ruth, after her mother-in-law's instruction, went to Boaz. She uncovered his feet and lay down by them. It was around midnight when Boaz awoke and noticed this strange woman at his feet. "Who are you?" he asked, not recognizing her in the darkness. "It is Ruth, your maidservant," she answered. Ruth continued by informing him that Naomi was kin to him thus making her kin, also.

The custom in those days was that when a woman lost her husband, a man who was next of kin was first in line to marry her. Ruth and Naomi intended to honor this. Boaz admitted to her that he was in fact "near kin," but there was another who was more closely related to her.

Boaz told her to sleep by his feet until morning but that she should leave before anyone recognized her. Ruth did so, leaving in the early twilight hours of the morning.

That day, Boaz filled her mantel, which she carried her grain in, as full as she could carry. He respected her for what she had done, caring for Naomi, even though she was not required to do so.

Evidently, Boaz had the future in mind, too. He had to investigate the matter of kinship. Did this other relative of Naomi want to marry Ruth? He set up a time to meet. When they met, the kinsman and the elders of the town were all present. Boaz laid his cards on the table. If the kinsman wanted to buy the land and property that belonged to Naomi, it was fine with him. He had to bear in mind that in purchasing the property, Ruth was considered part of it.

The kinsman refused to buy it and relinquished his right to it in the presence of the elders, which was the formal way of carrying out the act. Boaz quickly bought it all, including Ruth. "I have bought you to be my wife, to perpetuate the name of the dead in his inheritance, that the name of the dead may not be cut off from among his brethren," he stated. The deed was transacted, and God's will had been accomplished.

We note again that Jesus did not intend his lineage to be all from one nationality. He chose all kinds of people to fulfill the prophecies. Here we find that Ruth was a Moabitess, one of whom the Israelites often looked down upon as idol worshippers. Here is a woman chosen by God Himself to one day bring about the birth of the baby Jesus. Ruth gave birth to a son, who was named Obed, who was the father of Jesse, who was to be the father of David. It is from the house of David that the birth of Jesus was prophesied. So it was written, and so it was done.

ELI

In the book of Samuel, we read about a man named Eli. He was a godly man, a high priest and a judge of Israel. He was a very pious man, and it would seem that he had all the essential qualifications for his exalted offices. However, being human, he had one flaw.

The story of Eli is important. It should concern us because it demonstrates what God expects of us, especially fathers. We are reminded of the fact, which the Bible speaks about so much, that we must honor God with "fear and trembling."

Eli's two sons, Hophni and Phinehas, were being watched by God - a reminder to us that God indeed watches us. As is the case with so many of us, God didn't like what He saw.

Eli tried to be a good parent. Perhaps with all his duties, he may have neglected his obligations towards his family. We don't know for sure what happened. What we do know is that God judged him and his sons and disciplined all three. There was nothing Eli could do about it. All the offerings and sacrifices would do no good. It was too late.

The Bible says, *"The sons of Eli were worthless men"* (I Samuel 2:12)! I have heard it said many times, "The closer one is to the church, the further one is from the Lord." This is the case of the sons of Eli. Living in a rather holy environment, they rejected it. The fact is, the Bible declares, "They knew not the Lord."

When holy sacrifices were taking place, the boys robbed the Lord of His share of the peace offerings. Failing to follow the customs concerning offerings, they rebelled against it, seeking first the pleasure of their own luxury.

When women would come to do service at the tent meeting, going to church in other words, the sons of Eli would rape and seek pleasure with them any way they could. Imagine that: women going to church to serve God and being raped at the door! It was indeed an abomination to the Lord.

Eli had been informed of all the sins of his sons through the grapevine. Then the Lord sent another prophet to inform Eli of the upcoming doom concerning his sons. The Lord, through "this man of God," told Eli directly the problem He had with him. "He did not restrain his sons from blaspheming God," He said. Eli had an obligation that he did not fulfill.

Oh, yes, Eli talked to his sons after finding out their fate. Unfortunately, he was too meek and mild, much too gentle with them. He told them of the bad reports he had heard about them. He, more or less, warned them of the consequences, but he was not forceful enough. He failed to make the point. So instead, the prophet reproved Eli sharply and sternly.

When Eli was told his sons were to die young and on the same day, he seemed content in knowing that the Lord's will needed to be done. The day soon came when the two boys were killed in battle. To make matters worse, the Ark of God, a cherished, sacred memento of Sinai, which contained the tablets of stone, was also taken by the Philistines. When Eli heard this, he fell over backwards, broke his neck and was dead. The Lord's will had been done.

The wife of Phinehas was expecting a child. When she heard the news, her labor pains started, she gave birth and then died. But before she died, she made a statement, which was quite true. Being a gracious person, she loved her husband in spite of himself; she loved her father-in-law; but losing the Ark into the hands of the Philistines was too much. She said, "The glory has departed form Israel, for the Ark of God has been captured." The Ark, which had been symbolic of God being with Israel in all their troubles, was now gone. It looked hopeless. Little was she to know that in a short time, the Ark was to become a plague to the Philistines, and they returned it on their own.

The Lord had another plan going even while Eli lived to assure His will was done. Though Eli may have failed in some respects, he did not in others.

Samuel, whose mother was Hannah, a woman who had prayed for his arrival because she was barren, became a man of God. Hannah had gone to Eli prior to her becoming pregnant by her husband, Elkanah, crying to Eli about her problem. It was Eli who prophesied that she would bear a son because of her faith.

Eli taught Samuel the ways of the Lord. He was his mentor. When Samuel was a young lad, he heard a voice beckoning him, "Samuel, Samuel." Each time he heard it, he thought it was old Eli calling him. Eli, after the third time this happened, knew it was the voice of the Lord Himself and instructed Samuel to say, "Speak Lord for thy servant hears." From then on, Samuel listened to the voice of God.

Eli, though he failed as a father, served the Lord as a teacher. God continues to use us, even though we have our shortcomings.

SAUL

Now when Samuel grew old, his sons didn't like following after the Lord, either. The only punishment Samuel received from God was that the people of Israel demanded a king instead of a judge to lead their government. Samuel prayed for an answer, and the Lord told him to let the people have their king. The Lord, knowing the ways of the Israelites and Samuel's sons, told him to go ahead and let them have their way. Samuel warned the people of the demands a king would have over them. He would take their sons, daughters, land and possessions and would have them at his disposal. The people still wanted a king, so he had to find them one.

Samuel found a young, tall and handsome man. It appears as if Saul may have been a head taller than any other man. When he spotted Saul, the Lord told him, "Here is the man." Samuel anointed him with oil on the spot, making declaration of the Lord's intention. Soon the people would welcome Saul as their king.

It is said of Saul in I Samuel 10:9 that *"God gave him another heart."* When God calls an individual, this is what happens. You have another heart. Saul immediately had a new fire in his soul he had not had before. He wanted to tend to his people. God gave him wisdom to care about the Israelite nation. He was able to prophesy with the prophets of the era. With Samuel still acting as an advisor, Saul had an easy job of being a leader.

Even though Saul won many battles against his enemies, he was still just a man, and men have weaknesses. His weakness seemed to be pride. He was proud of what he was accomplishing, and it went to his head. When he led two hundred thousand men to defeat the Amalekites, he did not destroy everything, as God had intended, but saved it for himself, to make himself wealthier. Instead of bidding the Amalekites good riddance, he spared some, contrary to God's wishes, and God was displeased.

God was so unhappy with Saul that He was sorry He ever made him king, "for he has not performed My commands," He said. Saul, after being condemned by Samuel, appeared to be repentant. The Amalekite king, Agag, who Saul had spared to serve him, was brought before him. Saul cut him up in pieces as a gesture to prove to the Lord that he was sincere. But the Lord was not moved by his act.

Saul's pride and jealousy would get him into a lot of trouble later in life. When one of his leaders, like David, was more successful in battle than he was, he became angry and broke out in rages like a wild man would do. Whenever anyone would get more attention than Saul, that man would become his enemy. This became Saul's downfall. Once, when David returned from a battle, the people shouted, "Saul has slain his thousands, but David has slain his ten thousands." Saul couldn't stand having the people think more of someone else and often tried to kill the ones who got more attention than he. God was not happy!

When dealing with David, Saul was a politician. He would say one thing, tell David what he wanted to hear, and then do the opposite. Like people of today, when we sin, we often seek answers from astrologers and fortunetellers. Saul did the same. When Samuel died, it seemed that Saul was a lost man. He sought answers to his problems from witches. Finding no answers, Saul did what many do: he committed suicide. Saul fell on his sword and ended his life.

Saul's problems were brought upon himself. He thought too much of himself and not enough of God. When one thinks of what is best for him or herself, the results are often like Saul's. The life of Saul is one like so many of us have who delight in satisfying the pleasures of the body. The soul is neglected, not fed, and then starves to death. We become alienated from God and lost forever.

DAVID

If you have ever entertained the idea that God has no use for a sinner, you had better consider David. Although his life began quite purely, he made an about-face later in life - a life that could be an example for all of us, especially the worst of us.

The apostle Paul once referred to himself as "chief of sinners." David could also be considered as such. We need to take a closer look at this man, of whom Jesus is a direct relative. The Bible says from "out of the house of David" is where Jesus would be born.

Out of the gloomy, misty camp of war where King Saul was commander arose a young lad by the name of David. He was a shepherd boy, tending the flocks of his father, Jesse. David was called upon to soothe the temperament of his king. It seems that Saul would get himself into foul moods occasionally simply because "the Spirit of the Lord departed from Saul," the Bible says.

Listening to music would usually calm Saul down when he got upset. David, known for his artistic ability to play the lyre, or harp, was often summoned to play for Saul. During one visit to calm Saul's soul, a giant, by the name of Goliath was threatening the Israelite camp.

Every day, Goliath intimidated the Israelites by telling them that if one of their tribe would fight him and kill him, his tribe, the Philistines, would be their servants. No one challenged this huge mountain of a man, who stood nearly ten feet tall. Instead, they trembled in their sandals.

David heard the threats of Goliath. He asked, *"Who is this uncircumcised Philistine that he should defy the armies of the living God? Let no man's heart fail because of him, your servant will go and fight this Philistine"* (I Samuel 17:32)!

The word reached Saul that David was going to meet the challenge. Saul reminded David that he was just a child. David's three older brothers were already in his army. David was too young and too small to go to the army.

David gave Saul his resumé, so to speak. He reminded Saul how he had killed lions and bears, protecting his father's sheep. The Lord Who had delivered him then, would again deliver him from the hand of this giant.

Saul agreed, "and the Lord go with you," he said. Saul, not realizing the power that David had that day, wanted him to put on Saul's own armor. David couldn't handle it. It was too heavy, and he was not used to it.

Instead, he went to the nearby brook and gathered himself five smooth stones for his sling and approached the giant. Goliath made fun of him, looking down on this red-faced young lad. "Am I a dog that you come at me with sticks?" he inquired.

"You come to me with a spear and javelin, but I come to you in the name of the Lord of Hosts," was the shepherd boy's reply (I Samuel 17:43).

Goliath couldn't believe what he was seeing. A boy, whirling a sling around his head with a little stone in its pouch was going to kill him. Indeed!

With a smile on his face and laughing at his adversary, Goliath was in for the shock of his life – and the end of it. He could hear the whirring noise of the sling as David spun the sling over the top of his head. The heavy helmet that Goliath wore which protected his head from objects like swords and clubs was useless. A gap in the steel was located just above the bridge of his nose. This gap is more commonly known as "right between the eyes."

When David let the stone fly, it found its mark in the only vulnerable spot on the giant's body where there was no protection. With velocity near that of a small caliber rifle bullet, the stone sank deep into the forehead of Goliath. He fell like a tree that had just been cut, landing facedown.

David cut off Goliath's head as he had promised Saul. The Israelites, shocked at what they had witnessed, found a new spirit and rose up and fought the Philistines and routed them that day.

Saul, too, was amazed. He made David a leader of his army, but Saul soon became depressed and jealous of his new leader. David was very successful in his new role as soldier. He returned from battles victorious so many times that the people would shout, "Saul has slain his thousands, but David has slain his ten thousands." Saul couldn't tolerate someone being better than he and was afraid he would lose his kingdom to this young man who was more popular than he was.

Upon many occasions, Saul tried to kill this new threat to him. Each time, David would outsmart him. Saul gave David one of his daughters to marry, hoping to snare David that way so maybe one of the Philistines would kill him off guard.

In those days, David was required to give a gift to Saul prior to the wedding. Saul requested a hundred foreskins from the Philistines. Saul really hoped that David would be killed in the process. But David had the Lord on his side. He took his army and brought back two hundred foreskins. Saul continued to be David's enemy but couldn't go back on his word and allowed the marriage.

Saul's family even turned against him. His son, Jonathan, loved David like a brother and helped spare David's life. David's wife, Michal, also deterred her father from killing David. Everybody loved their new hero. No one wanted David dead. They protected him.

Saul ended up taking his own life one day during a battle after Philistine arrows had found their mark in his body. Rather than die by the hands of the Philistines, he fell on his own sword. The Lord had left him. He had no hope. His sons died with him in battle.

David prevailed. Now famous, he was anointed King of Israel. He was very successful. His love for music prompted him to write poetry, which are known as psalms today. He was a composer of the day, and his songs and words still live on to this day.

David would be tempted and tried like most of us who strive to serve the Lord.

One day, in the spring of the year, his army was out again fighting enemies. David remained in his house. While walking about on the roof, he noticed a beautiful woman bathing on another rooftop. Lust evidently filled his heart, and he wanted her. He was king, and he could have what he wanted. He sent for her, slept with her and she became pregnant.

She had a husband, Uriah, and he was a captain in David's army. When his wife, Bathsheba, had informed her king about her state, David tried to blame the pregnancy on her husband. David knew Uriah hadn't been home for quite some time, so he summoned Uriah home. When Uriah came home, he refused to leave his fighting men who were with him and chose to sleep with them as they did on the battle field. David tried to get him drunk so that he might go home and lay with his wife, but Uriah did not.

So what was the king to do? The only thing David could think of was to have Uriah killed. He arranged that Uriah be put in the battle front where the fiercest fighting was taking place so "that he may surely die." He did, and David thought he was in the clear—even though he now not only had committed adultery, but murder on top of it.

"Now the thing that David had done greatly displeased the Lord," the Bible says. David married Bathsheba. She was one more among his many wives, but she was different. Sin had brought them together. Bathsheba became a victim, and David a grave sinner.

To bring a person to repentance, God often provides someone to intercede. In this case, that person was the great prophet, Nathan. He went to David, who was unknowingly being set up by God Himself through His prophet. He told David a story, which went something like this:

There was once a rich man and a poor man. The rich man had many flocks and herds, but the poor man had only one ewe lamb to his name. The lamb ate with him, slept in the same room and was like one of the family. *It was like a daughter to him"* (II Samuel 12). The rich man had a house guest that evidently showed up unexpectedly. He was hungry from his travels and the rich man felt obligated to make him a meal. Instead of killing one of his own lambs to have for supper, he killed the one and only lamb that belonged to the poor man.

David listened for more, but Nathan had finished the story. "As the Lord lives, the man who has done this deserves to die," David angrily informed Nathan. It was terrible what the rich man had done. How selfish of the rich man, David no doubt thought.

Nathan looked David in the eye and stated, "You are the man!" The words must have hit David like a sledgehammer. What he had done with Bathsheba was the same thing. Nathan had given an excellent analogy of the entire ordeal. With much admonishment by Nathan, David was forced to his knees. "I have sinned against the Lord," he tearfully repented.

Nathan was stern with David, but assured him that he would not die but that his son would die as punishment for his great sin. David went through the rituals of repentance and begged God not to take his son born by Bathsheba, but God had made up His mind. The child died.

After a period of mourning, David came to grips with the situation. Still clinging close to God, in spite of himself, he never left His Master's side as some would have. He received comfort from God, and he made one of the most profound statements ever written in the Scripture. I have used it to comfort people in times of a loss of a loved one. He came to the conclusion that all his mourning could not bring his son back again. There was nothing he could do but live in this hope. *"I shall go to him, but he will not return to me!"* (II Samuel 12:23). Wow! What an assurance that we can all one day, God willing, be with our loved ones who passed on before us.

David was comforted, and he still had Bathsheba as his wife. He slept with her, and she had another son, Solomon, who would turn out to be one of Scripture's most successful individuals.

As for David, a grave sinner, he repented, paid the price and went on to become one of Scripture's greatest characters. His psalms have been used for centuries providing instruction, guidance, comfort and spiritual healing.

One psalm in particular, Psalm 51, has probably been used by more people throughout the ages than any other because we are all in need of its thoughts and words. David wrote it after the prophet, Nathan, convicted him of sin. In it are words that we can repeat to plead our case to the Lord God Almighty when we sin. It reads:

Have mercy on me O God, according to thy steadfast love; according to thy abundant mercy blot out my transgressions. Wash me thoroughly from my iniquity, and cleanse me from my sin. For I know my transgressions, and my sin is ever before me.

Against thee, thee only, have I sinned, and done that which is evil in thy sight, so that thou art justified in thy sentence and blameless in thy judgement.

Behold, I was brought forth in iniquity, and in sin did my mother conceive me.

Behold, thou desirest truth in the inward being; therefore teach me wisdom in my secret heart.

Purge me with hyssop, and I shall be clean; wash me and I shall be whiter than snow.

Fill me with joy and gladness; let the bones, which thou has broken rejoice. Hide thy face from my sins, and blot out all my iniquities.

Create in me a clean heart O God, and put a new and right spirit within me.

Cast me not away from thy presence, and take not thy Holy Spirit from me.

Restore to the joy of thy salvation, and uphold me with a willing spirit.

Then I will teach transgressors thy ways, and sinners will return to thee.

Deliver me from bloodguiltiness, O God, thou God of my salvation, and my tongue will sing aloud of thy deliverance.

O Lord, open thou my lips, and my mouth shall show forth thy praise.

For thou hast no delight in sacrifice; were I to give a burnt offering, thou wouldst not be pleased.

The sacrifice acceptable to God is a broken spirit, a broken and contrite heart, O God, thou wilt not despise.

Do good to Zion in thy good pleasure; rebuild the walls of Jerusalem, then wilt thou delight in right sacrifices, in burnt offerings and whole burnt offerings; then bulls will be offered on thy altar. (Psalm 51)

David sums it up. The way to repentance is to first, beg for mercy and ask for forgiveness. Second, we must ask to be cleansed.   Third, we must acknowledge our sin and recognize that only He can change the situation. Fourth, ask from Him Who is the Giver of all good things. The Bible declares that when we don't receive from God, "We have not, because we ask not!" Fifth, David asks to be kept close to Him, the God of his salvation, and ours, too. Finally, praise Him for his wonderful goodness, the reality of God making salvation possible for us.

We must realize that nothing we can do, like sacrificing, will make our relationship with God better. We must know that we have reached a point in our lives when we have perhaps reached a low, a humbling, that forces us to turn to God. A softening of the heart is what is needed before we can come to God. Then, and only then, will we have the assurance that God will not despise us.

He prays for the church, Zion, so they may not fall into the same sins as he did. Then David makes light of offering bulls on the altar, as was the custom in those days. Bulls were the costliest of all burnt offerings, and he acknowledges that all sacrifices are intended purely for the glory of God. When we have broken and contrite hearts, Almighty God will accept these sacrifices then. It is at that point when we, knowing what God has done for us, cannot help ourselves but to give Him the very best we have.

You have heard it said often, no doubt, that someone's "heart isn't right with God." Those pious individuals who are so good at judging others always seem to have it all figured out. They don't need a judging God. They believe they are capable of doing that all by themselves. They already know who is going to heaven and who is not. If you don't believe it, just ask them. They will be more than happy to tell you.

We cannot judge the proverbial book by its cover. What may appear sinful on the outside, probably is; but we don't always know where the heart is on the inside. We can't see that. Only God is capable of knowing.

David knew what was required to become "right" with God. We have his knowledge which he learned the hard way to show us the path we must follow. Follow the path David has shown us, and God will indeed be pleased with us. The Bible tells us so!

SOLOMON

You recall that it was our Lord Jesus Who made the statement, *"It is easier for a camel to go through the eye of a needle than for a rich man to enter the kingdom of heaven"* (Mark 10:25). Solomon, probably the richest man that ever lived, also struggled with that fact.

David, his father, was about to close his eyes in death. His son, Adonijah, wanted to be king, following in David's footsteps. Adonijah tried to self-appoint himself king prior to his father choosing him.

One of David's wives, Bathsheba, who he had committed a grave sin with, wanted her son, Solomon, to reign after David's death. She made David swear to it, and David followed through with his promise to her.

One can only imagine the dissension that prevailed with these two half-brothers, Solomon and Adonijah—especially with the latter, the brother who craved power. While Adonijah was already practicing his role as king, Bathsheba reminded David that Solomon was supposed to be the man for the job.

Solomon, sitting on his throne, couldn't tolerate this ambitious man, Adonijah. Solomon evidently foresaw trouble with him and had him put to death. Followers of Adonijah were also disposed of in some form or another—either driven out or killed. Solomon would not tolerate his enemies. It doesn't seem like the right thing to do, but Solomon got rid of them the quickest way possible, usually by death.

All great people have enemies. When one works for the public, all will not agree with that individual. The enemies of David were also killed and disposed of. Anyone who threatened the throne was quickly put to death. Those who had been kind to David, Solomon, in turn, was kind to them. It was not a democracy, and this is the way Solomon ruled his kingdom.

The Bible says, *"Solomon loved the Lord"* (I Kings 3:3). He followed in his father's footsteps and the Lord blessed him. In a dream one night, Solomon was asked by God, "Ask what I shall give you." The answer given by this new king was a humble one. He answered, "Give thy servant therefore an understanding mind to govern Thy people, that I may discern between good and evil."

The Lord was pleased with Solomon's request. Solomon did not ask for power and riches like most kings would, but he was asking for wisdom. God gave it to him.

Not long afterward, Solomon was tested. In I Kings 3, beginning with verse 16, two prostitutes brought an interesting case to Solomon's court. The two ladies were living together, and each had a baby. One of the children died. One prostitute claimed that the other had switched babies with her in the night. One was now childless. Each pleaded before Solomon that the living baby was hers.

Solomon picked up a sword and pretended he was going to cut the baby in half and divide it between the two women, knowing in his wisdom that the right mother would never allow her baby to be killed. He waited for the reaction. The real mother was quick to tell her king to just give the baby to the other woman just so it wouldn't have to be killed. Solomon knew then who the rightful mother was and restored her child to her.

The people were amazed by his wisdom in handling the situation of the two prostitutes and knew then that their king was indeed inspired by God. He gained much respect and later proved himself over and over again. It is written of him that "he was wiser than all other men." He was deemed the wisest man in the then-known world.

Around three thousand proverbs were uttered by this wisest of men - proverbs that attested to his fine wisdom. He wrote one thousand and five songs. In his writings, he spoke of nature, both fauna and flora. His wisdom became so much admired that people from all over the world came to listen to him.

Solomon had a mission. His father, David, was not allowed to build the great temple he wanted because of his sin. Solomon set out to do it. He made a treaty with an enemy nation, the Sidonians, because of the needed lumber that came from there. The temple that was erected using cedars from Lebanon. He traded with the Sidonians for the lumber, and they gained a peace that they had never known.

Solomon needed workers to build his great temple. He used forced labor. He made slaves out of his own people, and that probably didn't go over very well. Thirty thousand men went back and forth to Lebanon working with the lumber detail. He also had seventy thousand burden bearers to carry supplies. There were eighty thousand stone workers to carve the stone blocks and form the great slabs of stone. To oversee the operation, Solomon put thirty three hundred men in charge of seeing that the work was done.

This magnificent temple was second to none then and probably to this day, were it still standing.

Bigger temples have been built, but none this beautiful. It is said that it was sixty cubits long. A cubit is an ancient method of measurement, which involved the forearm of the builder, which varied from eighteen to twenty inches long. Assuming that his forearm was twenty inches, this would indicate that the temple was one hundred feet long. Using the same translation, it must have been around thirty-three feet wide and fifty feet tall, being several stories high.

While the temple was being built, there was never the sound of hammer or axe heard in the temple. All the material was formed and constructed away from the site, hauled in and assembled.

The inside of this structure must have been something to behold. The walls were boarded with cedar; the floors covered with cypress wood. Cedar was carved to depict fantastic art works of flowers and other assorted works. Gold was everywhere. Gold chains separated certain parts of the temple. The whole house was overlaid with gold. The altar, made of cedar, was overlaid with pure gold.

Carvings of cherubs made from olivewood graced the temple. Two cherubs, or angel-like figures, measured sixteen feet tall. Many such figures graced the temple. Altogether, it took seven years to build this great house of the Lord.

The word of the Lord had come to Solomon concerning His house. He would promise to dwell with the Israelites as long as they would follow His laws and commandments. This was a tall order for a nation that so often fell when it came to obeying the Lord.

Solomon continued in building up Jerusalem. He spent thirteen years building his own house, which was also very elaborate. All of the many palace buildings were constructed during this time, and every one of them was built with cedar and precious stones.

When the entire project was completed, Solomon dedicated it and gave a speech to the people praising God for the work that had been done. However, Solomon grew to love his riches, and it would become his downfall. The sin of pride very often becomes a stumbling block.

Before he realized he was on the wrong road, his riches had accumulated. The Bible tells us of his riches. To give us an idea of what he was worth, one must translate the talents into U.S. currency. Bear in mind that values do vary with currency. One talent of gold in those days equaled around $29,374. Solomon had 666 talents of gold. That adds up to nearly twenty million dollars! That was his personal income in one year derived from taxes, which, no doubt, were a burden upon the people. Additional tax revenue came from traders and merchants from far off countries that added to his wealth.

He had large shields of beaten gold—hundreds of them. His throne was made of ivory overlaid with gold. The finest of craftsmen were used to shape gold into statues of animals, such as lions. His drinking cups were gold. No silver was used; it wasn't good enough. Silver was as common in Jerusalem as stone. He owned fleets of ships that took him to various places of his kingdom.

He had fourteen hundred chariots and twelve thousand horsemen at his disposal. He would import chariots for six hundred shekels of silver - about $390 if a shekel is considered to be worth about 65¢. A horse was worth 150 shekels, or using the same value, about a hundred dollars.

Solomon also had many wives. The Bible says he had seven hundred wives and three hundred concubines. Concubines were women who lived with him, but he was not legally married to them. I suppose another word like "mistresses" could be used.

Just like Adam, Solomon's wives "turned away his heart," the Scripture says. He had made it a practice to marry foreign wives for political reasons. Marrying these women improved relations with foreign nations. He could get close to them and improve such things as trade, for example. But playing the political games turned out to be one of his downfalls in more ways than one.

With members of his household numbering in the thousands, just think of his grocery bill! The Bible says that to feed them all required three hundred bushels of flour, six hundred bushels of meal, ten head of fat cattle, twenty head of cattle taken off the grass, one hundred sheep, and on top of that, wild game was also prepared for the tables. All this for just one day's food supply.

Then consider what it would take to feed all his animals. First, he needed servants to do all the work. Then there were the acres of land and amounts of crops it would require to feed everything and everybody.

The biggest problem he had was trying to keep all his wives happy. Personally, I doubt it could be done. His wives, being from different parts of the earth, had many different types of gods they worshipped. They wanted to continue to do that even though they were married to the great Solomon. He was getting older and sought to please them all. His wisdom was leaving him.

When they wanted an altar built to worship their gods, Solomon had it done. This greatly displeased Almighty God. The Lord warned him, but it was already too late. Solomon had violated his covenant with God. He failed to keep his Father's statutes.

The punishment was severe. All that Solomon had worked for was ripped apart. Because he was David's son, God did not let it happen while Solomon lived. Knowing what would become of everything he worked for all his life surely caused Solomon great agony. After he was dead, everything he owned would be scattered in every direction, just because he forgot to honor his God.

I have seen this course of events happen in our times. I know of a family that "had it all." They were hardworking; they owned a lot of land; they had several sons to hand it all down to. They were very rich. Then in a moment of disregard as to where it all came from, they lost it all. The parents decided to experiment with wild living, consuming drugs and alcohol. They had what the Bible calls "a party spirit." They became involved in a crowd that took them for everything they had. They lost it all!

Possessions are temporary. When one fails to cling to the One Who allowed us to partake of it, we, too, can lose it all. It is far better to concentrate on something more permanent like loving God and the rewards that He gives us freely. The story of Solomon is in Scripture for our instruction. If we heed it, we won't end up like Solomon, who lost it all.

Jesus said it best when He stated, "Where your treasure is, that's where your heart will be also."

"The love of money is the root of all evil," writes the Apostle Paul. Keep in mind that it may not always be the "money" which causes us to sin, but the "love of it" is the cause of our problems. The Scriptures warn us of this and woe unto us when we fail to heed the inspired Word of God.

ELIJAH

After the death of Solomon, the kingdom of Israel was divided, just as God said it would be. Fighting and squabbling was the prominent situation of each day. These chosen people of God, Israel, were once again at war with themselves. Civil war, along with battles with foreigners, added to their distress.

Then God, Who always seems to set His Divine plan in motion, called on a man by the name of Elijah - a true man of God who wouldn't be swayed. He was so great that centuries later he appeared again at the mount of transfiguration with Christ Himself. Elijah, perhaps one of the Bible's greatest prophets, has a word for everyone, even today. He reminds me of John the Baptist with his apparel of camel's hair and leather.

Elijah was depressed, as we all become at times. He went to a cave to hide for he felt his own life was threatened by the Israelites. He admitted he failed in his fight to persuade the Israelite nation to turn back to God. He wanted to die and asked God to "take his life."

Many of us can relate to Elijah's predicament at this point in his life. But it is then that God often talks to us. We confess we are unworthy, and God comes to us, like He did with Elijah. He taught Elijah as He will teach us. I have stated in prior chapters that "God whispers to us in our happiness but He shouts to us in our pain." This is not always the case, however, as we see with Elijah.

God took Elijah outside of the cave as if to say, "I'm going to show you something." God did. He created a furious wind to blow, blowing so hard it literally crumbled the rocks on the mountain, blowing the mountain to bits. However, God was not there. He then created an earthquake, which shook the ground with great intensity, but again, God was not there. God created a fire that consumed everything in its path, and God was not there, either.

Elijah saw and heard the destruction that the Lord had created but noted that God wasn't there to comfort him. We would fail to find comfort in disasters that can happen in our lives, too, although they very often get our attention. They appear to be the Lord shouting at us.

But God chose to make Himself known to Elijah the next time by a whisper. The Bible calls it "the still small voice." This was not like the loud voice that boomed out from the mountain to Moses when he saw the burning bush. To Elijah, it was a whisper - perhaps intended to make him listen more closely. Although he had seen the terror of the Lord in the wind, earthquake and fire, he now saw the tender side of God portraying the Father image who takes his children aside and counsels them. God gave Elijah precise guidance as to what he must do next to straighten out the Israelites. Now armed with the "Sword of the Spirit," he is once again ready to do battle for the Lord. God's plan of preserving the remnant of Israel would take place through Elijah. Elijah would not do it alone any longer.

Traveling down the road, he saw a man in the field plowing with twelve yoke of oxen. The man's name was Elisha. Elijah, as a symbol of having Elisha take Elijah's place in the future, threw his coat around Elisha.

We must think about this for a moment. Here is one of the first examples of someone following God from another's invitation. Elisha was what some would consider a big farmer. He probably thought a lot of his farming operation. He had a family, and he was asked to leave and follow after Elijah. He had to decide if he wanted to leave it all and is given a brief period to think about it. He asks if he can say goodbye to his parents, and Elijah allows it. Elisha even killed the oxen and had them prepared as a feast with his family as he departed them. He didn't sell them, like most of us would do today, but he literally destroyed them. He couldn't farm without them and knew he no longer needed them. He could not help himself. The spirit of Elijah was now with him when the mantel, or coat, fell upon Elisha's shoulders. God called him, and he accepted the call.

"The still small voice" summons each and every one of us. Some think of it as the Holy Spirit or conscience ministering to us. Others believe they see or hear the works of God somewhere in their daily lives. In some form or another, God truly speaks to us today. I have heard Him and so have you if you listened closely. The still small voice is what you heard and may not have believed it.

I have witnessed this voice myself. It's probably why I believe in it so strongly. I believe in prayer, which I define as a talk from the heart with God. I speak; He listens. I keep quiet; He talks to me. I have my own private place where I go to be with God. It's not in a church, as some people believe is the proper place to talk to God, and I don't argue that. As a matter of fact, that's great. But for me, I have to go somewhere where I know I will not be interrupted. Since I live on a farm, we have ponds in the pastures. It's very quiet and serene out there.

It's where I go when I am troubled and need to visit with my Creator.

I have even gone so far as to construct a little altar out of red rocks native to the area. The Bible says many different times that when an individual had a talk with God, that individual would build an altar no matter where he was. It's a form of acknowledging your intentions, I believe. While some would consider it silly, I deem it necessary.

Anyway, while I kneel there with nature all around me, it's easy to feel God's presence. The birds singing, wild flowers blooming and small creatures around me makes me realize Who is in charge. I am humbled at His mighty works, and I am in awe as to what a loving God we have. During the day, I look up to the sky where I see the clouds and the sun. At night, I view the moon and stars that grace the heavens and I ask myself, "How can anyone say there is no God?" He's all around me!

As we have our talk, I note the waves in the water a few feet from me. When I speak, the water turns calm as if He's listening to me. When I am quiet and wait for His answer or reply, a gust of wind creates little waves in the water. I know that He is there because it continues to occur. Quiet, and then a breeze, over and over again. It's as if the breath of God comes across the waters and ministers to me. I hear the still small voice and yes, it is a whisper, in the form of a gentle breeze, which brings my soul solace unlike I have ever known.

I am reminded of the song, "In the Garden," where "He walks with me and He talks with me." It's real, I guarantee it. He tells me that I, in spite of myself, am His very own. That's assurance. It's what I need often in life, more than I like to admit.

Why did I bring up Elijah? We don't learn much from him because of sin unless we use the depression he went through over Israel. It was a sin to worry and is yet today. The point is, Who did he go to? He didn't try to find the answer at the bottom of a bottle or a package of pills. He went to the Top, to the Lord God Himself to find answers.

Elijah is a tremendous example of what we all need to do. We need to listen for the Voice that speaks to us and make our peace with God. We need to listen to His instructions like Elijah did, and we will all get along a whole lot better in life. It's a promise - one promise of around three hundred in the Bible given by God. God doesn't break His promises. Go to Him , and He will answer you. Just prepare yourself to listen, and you will hear the Voice in some form or another.

You may even be fortunate enough to have someone cast their coat on you and ask that you leave it all and follow Him. What a wondrous opportunity that would be! There are many people I have spoken with over the years that tell me, "I think I had a call one time," but they failed to heed it. All kinds of experiences have and are still happening today, and we wonder, could it have been a call from the Master Himself? Listen and listen good. It may be just a whisper or may be with a tremendous awakening. One way or another, God will speak to us and confirm our call. Are you ready to listen?

ELISHA

I feel compelled to make note of Elisha as well. This great prophet could probably be called one of the greatest. Why? Simply because he asked for, and received, a double portion of Elijah's Spirit.

When it became time for Elijah to leave this earth, he, like his great ancestor Enoch, who walked with God, did not die. God simply took him up to heaven on a chariot of fire. Elisha was a witness to the event and just prior to Elijah taking his leave, Elisha asked his for an inheritance. "I pray you, let me inherit a double share of your spirit," he asked.

Elijah in turn assured him that if he saw him going up into heaven to be with his Lord, his petition would be granted. The chariot and horses of fire, carrying his great mentor, went up like a whirlwind towards the heavens. Elisha saw it all.

Being a Godly man, Elisha, like his forerunner Elijah, performed a great many miracles and acts of kindness. He healed and restored life. He restored unity between nations, and God was with him.

Perhaps one of his greatest examples of Godliness occurred when the Syrian army attempted to capture this man of God. He was accused of helping the king of Israel outwit the Syrians. Elisha had evaded them many times, and this seemed to be a challenge to the captain of the army. He learned where Elisha was staying and surrounded the city one night. In the morning, one of the servants noted the predicament. They couldn't fight them off because of the numbers, and there was no way out. All they could do was give themselves up to the mercy of the Syrians.

Elisha looked at the scene in a different sense. People of God always tend to look at the bright side. He made a statement that soldiers in recent wars still recall. They, when all looked lost, remembered the Bible stories they had heard when they were little boys. A new sense of victory filled their spirit and the battle was won.

Elisha's comment was simply this: "Fear not, for those who are with us are more than those who are with them." He did not depend upon his own strength but the power of Almighty God to deliver him once again. He realized the Power he had at his disposal, and we should learn from him. God has promised that His angels will look out for us in times like this. All that needed to be done was ask, and ask is what Elisha did. The words of the New Testament could also be used here. "If God be for us, who can be against us."

"Strike these people with blindness," he prayed. The Lord heard his prayer, and the entire Syrian army was immobile. They were now at the mercy of the Israelites. Elisha led the Syrians to the King of Israel who wanted to kill them all. If Elisha would have asked God to kill them on the spot, He would have done it. Elisha had foreseen that forgiveness was the answer and sent them all back to their homeland with their vision restored. They never wanted to raid the camps of the Israelites again.

One incident that happened after he died was rather interesting. It concerned a man who had died and was hastily buried in the same sepulcher as Elisha. When his body touched the bones of Elisha, life was restored to his body. Even in death, Elisha's power was still at work.

The Scripture makes note of the fact that Elisha died because of a sickness. We don't know what it was, but he was at a ripe old age, his work was done, and he died. Just because you or a loved one loves God, it doesn't exempt of us from the calamities of life. Elisha wasn't exempt either. Nonetheless, the great prophet was honored in his life and in his death. We can only hope for the same.

JOB

If you have ever suffered to some extent, you have probably heard or read the story of Job. God tested this great man, whom the Bible declares was "blameless and upright." Satan set up the challenge, and God allowed it to happen. This is important to remember in our own lives.

Here's the set-up. Satan and the Lord had a talk about Job. The Lord had blessed Job greatly. He was very rich and had a nice family. Satan knew that, but he more or less made a bet with God that if Job was afflicted with all kinds of misfortune, he would forget God and curse Him. God, knowing the heart of Job, let the devil have him, except Satan was not to kill Job. The devil was given a limited time to have his ways done in Job. A true man of God cannot be moved, at least not completely.

First, a great wind came and destroyed Job's house and all his sons and daughters that were inside it. He lost what was most important to him, his children. Then he lost all his livestock, which were many. Most were stolen by thieves. Job's response was simply, "Naked I came from my mother's womb, and naked I shall return. The Lord gave, and the Lord has taken away. Blessed be the name of the Lord." He had lost his children and his means of income, and yet he did not curse God.

The devil wasn't content with that. He figured Job had not suffered enough and would fall if he had. God allowed Job to be afflicted with sores from the soles of his feet to the top of his head. He hurt so bad, that his wife even wondered why he would not just curse God and die.

Job had three good friends. His friends were people we can relate to because they thought as many of our friends would today when things look bleak. They all felt that all of Job's sufferings were because of his sins. How quickly people tend to attempt to figure out God's divine plan and pass judgment on towards their friends. They were telling Job that nobody suffers unless they have sinned. Job denied it and knew how upright he was. He perhaps knew that this was only a test. His friends thought he just needed to get right with God. Job wondered what more he could do. An argument among the friends developed because Job would not be moved from his faith and trust in God.

His friends provoked Job's thoughts, however. Job began to question theological truths. He acknowledged that people are born into troubles. He also knew that God promises deliverance. In his weakness, he asked God to let him die, but continued in prayer. He upheld God's justice and stood firm to his innocence. His friends urged him to repent, but Job resented their words, and he defended his integrity. He searched his soul for the answers and asked, "If a man die shall he live again?" He humbled himself, and finally his three friends and wife deserted him completely.

He was moved to ask God as to why the wicked never seem to suffer. They never seem to lose anything but enter Sheol, or hell, in peace. He learned that the wicked will receive their reward eventually.

Job also discovered more about himself, as we all must do during times of pain. We all wonder what has happened just like this man of God. He searched for wisdom from God so he would be able to sort things out. One statement he made is astounding and is quoted often to this day. *"The fear of the Lord, that is wisdom. And to depart from evil, that is understanding,"* Job realized (Job 28:28).

Finally, another one of Job's friends couldn't keep silent any longer. Because he was younger than Job, he felt that it wasn't his place to butt in on the conversation Job and his other so-called friends were having. His name was Elihu. After hearing both sides of the story, Elihu became angry with the three friends and also with Job. He accused Job of justifying himself rather than God, and accused the three friends for not finding an answer to Job's problems. How nice it was to finally have a mediator who could set everyone straight.

Elihu affirmed that God often does use pain to chastise His people in order to bring them back to the fold. He declared that God is never unjust and always understanding. He warned Job of being a proud man and that he should not pass judgment on men, always bearing in mind to praise the work of God. Elihu was acting as a messenger of God, and Job listened to him. Elihu had affixed in Job's mind that suffering is God's way of strengthening and purifying his children—a way of bringing them even closer to Him.

Job humbled himself and listened to God speak in a whirlwind and was reminded of man's limited knowledge. God explained to him all the wonders of animal life. Who knows the secrets of the Most High? Job repented and acknowledged he didn't know much, nor did he understand the works of God. God forgave him and everything was restored to him that was taken away. The Bible says he received twice as much as he had before. He had it all back again and then some.

Job was not without sin; he was just a man. Perhaps he was guilty of the sin of pride and passing judgment on others too quickly. We are no different. The lessons we learn from the story of Job are ones we can take to the bank, so to speak. Assuming that Job's three friends were God-fearing people, they evidently didn't know much either. A younger man is who God used. We generally believe that younger people aren't supposed to have much wisdom. In this case, one who wasn't supposed to have much wisdom seemed to have the answers. We must be watchful when it comes to advice we get from others. Once again, we must listen to God when He speaks to us and carry out His plan for our lives. He may restore that which was lost and like Job, maybe twice as much.

Yes, perhaps we will suffer in life or already are suffering. There is a reason, no doubt. Whatever that reason is, we must individually understand and act accordingly. I, like many, find it hard to realize what the purpose is many times. To see an innocent child suffer is beyond my understanding. But then, who am I? I'm no more intelligent than this man of God named Job. We have a lot to learn and perhaps not much time to do it in. We may be tempted to ask, "Where is God," when it happens. Listen, He is there. He may be at the door, knocking. All we need to do is let Him in.

The apostle Paul sums it up best. *"I consider that the sufferings of the present time are not worth comparing with the glory that is to be revealed to us"* (Romans 8:18). Often it is through suffering that

God does indeed reveal Himself and make His presence known to us.

THE PREACHER

After the death of Solomon, we find another book he wrote, probably in his old age. The book, of course, is Ecclesiastes, or "The Preacher," as it is referred to. Apparently, Solomon saw the folly of his riches, power and his life work of striving to attain "things," so he wrote about it. This is a great story for each and every one of us to ponder, although it must be read in its entire context to realize the full effect of the wisdom of Solomon.

In the beginning of the book, it is very easy to think that these are the writings of a genuine pessimist. "Everything is vanity," or of no use. "What good is anything?" he asks us. We work hard, become tired and what good has it done for us? Generations come and generations go, and the earth remains. What difference did we make? When we are gone, who cares? He paints a dismal picture of our lives.

He goes on to say that he realizes now that there is no pleasure in wealth: we are all going to die and the saying, "you can't take it with you," is the bottom line. He says he enjoyed himself, but it brought him no lasting pleasure. He notes that he tried to find pleasure in fine wine, like many who believe having a good time is found in the bottom of the bottle. Solomon says that pleasure is not there!

He tells of all his accomplishments: building cities, owning lots of land and livestock. He says he had much silver and gold and the pleasures of concubines. Yet, what good was it? It has been said about Moses that he denied to become involved in the "pleasures of sin for season." Solomon partook of it. He had it all! And now that he was reflecting upon it, he came up empty. Something was lacking. The Spirit of God was not always in his life. Without God, life is vanity, he admits.

Perhaps one of the chapters which has induced more thought than anything else he ever wrote is the third chapter of Ecclesiastes, where he talks about there being "a time for everything." "For everything there is a season," he states. He continues to elaborate on the subject. I'm going to quote his first eight verses because I think they are something we need to ponder, too.

A time to be born, and a time to die.
A time to plant, and a time to pluck up what is
planted.
A time to kill, and a time to heal.
A time to break down, and a time to build up.
A time to weep, and a time to laugh.
A time to mourn, and a time to dance.
A time to cast away stones, and a time to gather
stones together.
A time to embrace, and a time to refrain from
embracing.
A time to seek, and a time to lose.
A time to keep, and a time to cast away.
A time to rend, and a time to sew.
A time to keep silence, and a time to speak.
A time to love, and a time to hate.
A time for war, and a time for peace.
(Ecclesiastes 3:1-8)

There is, indeed, a time for everything. There is a reminder here that things constantly change. We live in a changing world, and we must prepare to go along with it. With God, the transitions in life are easy, but without Him, the roads to change are rough, and everyone doesn't make it.

Life is tough; Solomon knew this all too well. He's "been there, done that." He does not hesitate to continually remind his readers of the vanity of being wealthy. He goes so far as to say that the poor man enjoys a better night's sleep than the rich man because the rich man lays awake nights worrying about losing his wealth or thinking how to make more. "Naked he came from his mother's womb, and naked he will leave, taking nothing with him," he establishes.

Jesus once told the story of a rich man who was called by his Master to follow Him, but he could not. He had many possessions and didn't want to leave them. They were too important to him. He enjoyed them to such a great extent that he chose them rather than God. "Woe unto them," the Bible warns us with reference to people like that.

Solomon realized that and preaches it to us. He tells us that a "good name" is more important than all the riches in the world. Trying to be a wise person is often folly in the eyes of God, he tells us. Many times, we wonder about all the "whys" of life. Why do we suffer? Why am I poor? Why am I oppressed? Why am I sad all the time? Solomon reminds us that these problems are often put there to make us better individuals. During these times is when we most often turn to God, and He counsels us. We become closer to Him. Solomon knew that when he was so-called "happy," gloating in his possessions, God was farther away from him. God was not actually far away, but Solomon was far from God. We tend to forget God during the happy times of our lives.

Solomon tells us that it pleases God when we make the best out of life as long as God is in the midst of it. Eat, drink and be merry, as long as God has approved of what you are doing with your life. Enjoy your spouse, family and what God has given to you. "Whatever your hand finds to do, do it with all your might," he says. This is good advice when God is in what we do.

In this book of lessons, Solomon teaches us that charity is very important. The God who gives to us liberally expects us to give to the less fortunate. Many times, the rich tend to get greedy and share little. This is not pleasing to God. To most theologians, "Cast your bread upon the waters," is referring to the charitable individual. They sow more than they will use for themselves. Some of their excess is intended to be shared - part of our "good works." God requires us to share with others from the abundance that we may have.

I knew of an elderly lady who lived in her home with only her meager social security check to live on each month. Yet, she shared with others. If someone needed a dollar, she had it for them. She would bake and share with the needy. She thought more of others than she did of herself. She was indeed a Christian, and one could see it by her good works.

How are people going to know that we are Christians except by our good works? Not that it is going to gain us a seat in heaven: Jesus did that on the cross. The Bible says that whatever we do, it is because of the love of God in our hearts, and we are "constrained" to do what is right in the sight of God. We simply cannot help ourselves. We have to do it.

We need this Spirit of God living in us which tells us what to do each and every day.

Solomon realized this in his old age, apparently. He reminds us, "Remember your Creator in the days of your youth." When we are young, we are often full of ambition, which we should be. However, we often forget God, as Solomon admits. How much better and happier we would be when we are young to walk in the ways of the Lord and prosper and enjoy life. This is acting wisely, as Solomon stresses.

"Fear God, and keep His commandments, for this is the whole duty of man," he concludes in Ecclesiastes 12:13. If we follow the advice of Solomon, we should be truly blessed both while we live and when we are gone. It's not so hard. When we love God, it's easier to do the things He expects of us. As I said before, we cannot help ourselves than to want to please Him. It's what we are all about.

Solomon often referred to the relationship with God as a father and son relationship. The father loves his son and the son, the father. Neither one ever wants to make the other unhappy. They conduct their lives pleasing one another because they love one another. Such it is with a firm relationship with God. He loves us and wants the best for us, much like our parents did. Although parents sometimes have flaws, God does not. He loves us with an everlasting love, an "agape" love, which never fails even when He may be unhappy with us. And who among us does not want to make our parents proud of us? It is because we love them. How great it is when God is indeed proud of us. That's a relationship!

THE PROPHETS

There is not much that can be learned from the sins of the prophets because they committed few. Most were very Godly individuals. They were important in Biblical times—they were the "Bibles" of the early followers of God. They spoke the words given to them by Almighty God Himself. God spoke to them in many different ways; visions, dreams and voices being the most common. Like Elijah and the "still small voice" he heard, many times this is how the words of God were conveyed to others. They had no Bibles then, of course, but these great prophets gave the Word literally.

These were men like Isaiah, who began his work over seven hundred years before Christ led nations and individuals to the paths they were to follow—paths the Lord wanted them to be on. Isaiah even predicted the coming of Jesus Christ centuries before He came. They knew what they were talking about. In Isaiah 53, he states, *"Surely He has borne our griefs and carried our sorrows. He was wounded for our transgressions, He was bruised for our iniquities."* He refers to Christ who did it all for us.

People today suspect there are prophets at work. I believe there are some, but at the same time, we must be aware of the false prophets the Bible warns us about. Those that tell us when the world will end noting the hour of the day, even, can be discounted. No one knows when the end will come, save God alone. The Bible tells us that! Many different types of would-be prophets are alive and well today, and they often mislead people to destruction. Mass suicides have taken place because of some of those who believed so strongly to follow

98

the false prophet, they were misled to the very ends of the earth. They were deceived, and the Bible warns us of those individuals. It instructs us that they will appear as wolves in sheep's clothing. "Beware," we read of these types of prophets.

Prophets appear to have been called at all stages of their lives. Isaiah was evidently married already when the word of the Lord came to him. Men like Jeremiah were young. He was so young, in fact, that he doubted anyone would listen to him.

"Before I formed you in the womb, I knew you," said Jeremiah of the word of God that came to him. Before he was born, God chose him! God assured him that even though he was young, *I am with you to deliver you,* promised the Lord (Jeremiah 1).

Jeremiah had a difficult task. God's chosen people, the Israelites, could not stay on track. They wandered off of it so many times, and each time a prophet had to shake them up really hard. Constantly, they would worship other gods and forsake their Lord. They were punished very bitterly at times to get them to "turn around" or repent. They were a people that demonstrated weakness very much, like most of us today. We have the Bible; they had the prophets.

Unlike the Bible, which never falters, these prophets of old were human, and often found it hard to continue with their work. They became depressed, like Jeremiah. This prophet of doom, as he is referred to, feared for his life most of the time. People didn't like what he told them. They feared him. He became a weeping prophet, often feeling so sorry for himself that he literally wanted to die. Although he was lonely, misunderstood and persecuted for his efforts, he remained true to God. He is a shining example for our own lives, although we may not consider ourselves prophets.

Men, like Ezekiel, had visions. Visions are often hard to understand and are often misinterpreted. John, in the Book of Revelations, is another example of a man who had visions. God gives visions which are there for a purpose and to confuse man, I often think. John tells his stories and prophecies like the true visionary person he was. One can imagine him sitting there reciting the vision God had given Him, no doubt looking upward towards the heavens as he pronounces God's plans. People often doubted these types of prophets, but their verdict was certain. What they said, God meant.

In his thirty-fourth chapter, Ezekiel talks about the search for lost sheep, much like Jesus did years later. He speaks of them being scattered, as the Lord God had instructed him to say. He tells how he fed and nurtured them, with all reference being made to the children of Israel. They were the sheep who had continually gone astray. Like the prophet Isaiah also gave reference to, "All we like sheep have gone astray." This is a verse that is quoted over and over again to remind the fallen sinner that he or she can be found and brought back into the Master's fold.

Another prophet who could interpret visions was Daniel. Those of us who went to Sunday School all recall the story of Daniel. He was our hero. He was the man who was in the lion's den and was spared because God shut the lions' mouths.

Ezekiel referred to him as an example of righteousness and wisdom, which Daniel certainly was.

One notable explanation of Daniel's ability to interpret things from God was when he pronounced judgment on King Belshazzar who reigned over Babylon at the time. Babylon was a wicked nation. Mysterious handwriting had appeared on the wall of the king's palace. No one could understand what it meant. Daniel was summoned because he had been recognized for his interpretation abilities.

The writing read, "MENE, MENE, TEKEL, and PERES." "The handwriting was on the wall," is the phrase often used today to describe a prophetic event.

Daniel's interpretation is for all of us, not merely for the king of Babylon. Daniel explained the words: MENE—"God has numbered the days of your kingdom and brought it to an end." TEKEL—"You have been weighed in the balances and found wanting." PERES—"Your kingdom is divided and given to the Medes and the Persians." Daniel was right—the kingdom fell just like he said it would. Belshazzar was slain that very night. He had no more opportunities to repent. His life was over.

These words have meaning for us. Often we think we have it quite comfortable, forgetting God and our duty towards Him. The question we must ask ourselves is will God take it away from us because of our vanity. We, too, will be weighed in the balances one day, and we must pray that we are not found wanting. If we are, what will become of us? Perhaps we all need to quiz ourselves and see where we would stand before a living God.

Now, Daniel was a bold man. It took nerve to continue living in the heathen nation of Babylon. Often, even today, one has to go where sin abounds to eliminate it. Daniel was alone when he worshipped the God of his ancestors. He would pray at least three times a day, and his enemies made note of it. They thought it wasn't right that he lived among them and didn't worship their gods. They reported it to the king, Darius, who liked Daniel. No doubt, Darius could see the fine qualities of Daniel and respected him. However, due to public pressure, the king had to resort to the rules and cast Daniel into a lion's den. Daniel had Darius thinking and one could say at this point, like King Agrippa Paul talks about that he, *"Was almost a Christian"* (Acts 26:28).

When morning came, King Darius, who had worried all night about Daniel, still hoped Daniel was alive. Something told the king that God would take care of Daniel. Opening the den, he shouted for Daniel. "Has your God who you serve continually delivered you from the mouths of the lions?" the King asked anxiously.

Immediately came the response from Daniel. "My God sent his angel to shut the lion's mouths and they have not hurt me for God has found me blameless and also before you, O king, I have done no wrong!"

King Darius knew Daniel was right. He had done no wrong. He sent for those who accused Daniel of this alleged wrongdoing of praying to his God. He had them, along with their families, thrown into the den of hungry lions. The victims were thrown to the lions from a door in the ceiling. It is written that the lions tore them to pieces before they touched the ground.

It took a miracle for King Darius to truly acknowledge God, but he did. He made a decree that all his nation was to fear God, the God of Daniel. The king recognized God's power.

Oh, I have heard it said so many times, "If only I could see a miracle, I would believe in God." You did, and you have! You just read about one. That's not enough, you say? Perhaps your eyes have not been opened, nor your heart softened to the living God. Perhaps you wouldn't see a miracle if it "bit you in the nose," as the saying goes. Jesus said, "Blessed are they who believe and have not seen!" We have all experienced miracles and great things, but we just don't give God the credit.

Who do you suppose makes it possible for the sun to come up each morning and display it's beauty in the sunrise? Who do you suppose is in charge of all nature? Who instills in the birds the instinct to migrate? The list could go on and on. Man certainly doesn't do it and isn't capable of it. I believe it is, indeed, God who placed all planets in our solar system "with his fingertips." He is in charge. No one else could have done it. No cosmic force, or anything else, can match the power of God. Even a learned man like Einstein, a physicist, stated, "I want to know God's Father!" All the knowledge in the world cannot disprove God Almighty, and he knew it. Remember, he was a smart man. How about you?

God has a plan: He has always had a plan for people. Look for a moment at the prophet, Hosea, one of twelve minor prophets. He was instructed via a vision of God that he should marry Gomer, a local prostitute. Hosea didn't like the idea, but nevertheless, he did as God instructed him. It was not a sin for Hosea to marry her, but what was God wanting to prove? He wanted to show the Israelites that they were doing the same thing. They were living in sin like the prostitute - prostituting themselves to the point of no return. Gomer was the sinner and so was Israel. They needed to witness an analogy through His prophet, Hosea.

God drove His point home hard so that all the people could see the error of their ways. God has to do that sometimes. The first child of Hosea and Gomer was a son. God told them to name him Jezreel which signifies dispersion and the shedding of blood of the house of Jehu. Israel would again witness division and death.

With the birth of their second child, a girl, God told Hosea to name her "Not pitied." No longer would He take pity on the house of Israel. He had enough of their backsliding. Like Paul wrote to the Romans, "God gave them up" due to their wicked ways of living.

The couple had another son whom the Lord named "Not my people" because He continued to drive His point home that He had every intention of abandoning them. They were not His people anymore. Only the tribe of Judah remained true to Him. God would eventually separate the tribe of Judah from His once-chosen people. They had been more faithful than the other ten tribes of Israel. Historically, God had always shown mercy to the tribe of Judah.

Then God appears to have changed His mind concerning the Israelites. He can do that, He's God! Controversy takes place among theologians as to when Israel was reunited. Remember, God made a promise to His people, Israel, and He isn't One to break His promises. He does as He pleases to bring those who have strayed back into the fold. Sometimes, it appears as if He has to scare them a little. They knew better than to sin, and they knew the consequences of it. Yet, they chose to live in this state of "prostitution" when they knew better. Eventually, they became one again with the tribe of Judah.

Many think that the time of being reunited took place when the ten tribes returned from Babylonian captivity. Others think it didn't take place until Christ Himself came upon this earth and made reference to Jew and Gentiles. The first disciples of Christ were partly Jews, or Israelites, and partly Galileans. Whatever the case, they were eventually reunited again. Christ was, and is now, the Savior of all people.

The point is, as is recorded in the last chapter of Hosea, they must repent. "Return O Israel to the Lord your God." Quit selling yourselves out, God is telling them. Wicked as they were, they had plenty of opportunities to repent and return to the Lord. We, who stumble and fall, can do the same. "God who is faithful and just will forgive our sins." It's a promise!

As time passed, other prophets continued to stress repentance to the children of Israel. Joel was one; Amos was another. Many Jews believe that Amos had a burden. He is believed to have been a country farmer and had a speech problem - stuttering. It was an extra burden to him, but God chose him, proving He can use anybody. Amos could have been a man like Moses who it is said couldn't speak well, either.

How often do we hear the excuse, "I can't speak in public or speak in front of a crowd." You can do it if God has need of you. I have lived with it for over fifty years, and He has used me a lot.

JONAH

I like this guy, Jonah. I can relate to him. It's why I have given him a chapter of his own. Many of us are often just like him - trying to hide from God; not wanting to do His will even though we know what it is.

Jonah is not more popular than the rest of the prophets, but I would imagine his story, written by his own pen as some claim, is the most controversial. Here's a guy who is swallowed up by a whale and lives inside the animal for three days and nights. Jesus referred to Himself as one, who like Jonah, would spend three days and nights in the belly of the earth. Many skeptics of Biblical writings think this whole story is nonsense, saying no one could survive long inside a fish. Jonah says he did. I believe it happened since the Bible is the inspired word of God. With God, nothing is impossible. Scientists even have had to admit that in some species of these great mammals, there is an air chamber located in the upper part of the neck where one could survive. However he did it, he did survive, because God had a mission for him.

The story unfolds in Jonah, chapter 1, where Jonah is instructed by God to go to Nineveh, a Gentile city of 120,000 people and a lot of livestock. Jonah was to preach the word of God to every soul. They were wicked, worshipping other gods and forsaking the God of Jonah. He knew that, and he was prejudiced against them - a downfall of Jonah's.

Jonah didn't want these people to know the Lord. He wanted them to destroy themselves in their ignorance. God, on the other hand, Who does not

106

wish that anyone perish in their sin, wanted Jonah to preach repentance to them and turn them around. Jonah tried to hide from his Lord by boarding a ship at Joppa which was going to Tarshish, which was in the opposite direction of Nineveh. He foolishly crawled down in the bottom of the ship hoping to hide from God. I am astonished that he didn't know better. God always knows where you are. Jonah was a prophet, for goodness sake. Perhaps he did know better and his prejudice concerning the wickedness of this city overpowered his thinking. There was no way that he was going to preach to them, he didn't even like them. He despised them.

He was on the ship, which was not a large one, and God made a wind storm happen. The ship and it's crew were bobbing around the Mediterranean Sea like a cork. The lumber was creaking and groaning with each mighty wave that slapped against it. Water was coming over the deck. Jonah, thinking he was hidden from God, was fast asleep below the deck.

The sailors were rowing for all their worth, yet they couldn't get the boat under control. Each one prayed to his own god, and nothing happened. Finally, the captain went below and found Jonah fast asleep. The captain woke him up and asked him to pray to his God before they all perished.

By then, the crew was convinced that it was Jonah who was causing the storm. They quizzed him, and Jonah admitted that it was his fault. He told them to throw him overboard, and the storm would cease. The crew, who were good men, didn't want to do that, so once again they rowed all the more persistently but to no avail. They finally decided to listen to Jonah and throw him overboard.

A great fish swallowed him in order to spare his life. God arranged that, too, of course. The Bible says He "appointed" this fish. Imagine that. God controls the animals as well as us if we let Him.

I heard a story one time about a man who was being attacked by a mountain lion in the Rocky Mountains in Colorado. From out of nowhere came a dog who deterred the lion long enough for the man to escape. Could it be that God appointed dog, too? No one ever knew if the dog belonged to anyone or not. There was no one else in the area. He may have been a stray that Almighty God stationed there for a purpose. That purpose was accomplished, for the man became a believer and served God the rest of his life.

Back to the story. Jonah was inside the fish. Wherever the fish went, Jonah went - on the surface of the water and down to the very depths of the sea. He had time to think about what he had done. The great thing about Jonah is the fact that he finally admitted his mistakes. I can respect anyone who does that.

He prayed, and three days later the fish, by some miracle, spit him out on the coast and on dry land. I wonder what Jonah was feeling at that time. Was it one big belch and out he came? However the act was done, which is not important, God shows us that there is a resurrection for those who repent. Jonah did, and he more or less "rose again" to fulfill his mission.

Jonah walked to Nineveh and began his sermons. Jonah was a very eloquent speaker. He was a gifted orator and was very convincing with his words. He told the Gentiles that unless they, too, repented that they would perish in forty days. The amazing thing is that people listened. They, too, saw the errors of their ways and turned to God. He spared this large city. If the had not repented, they may have ended up like Sodom - burned to the ground along with every living thing in it.

In order to get people's attention, I once heard that the miracle of Jonah and the whale was not the real miracle of the story. The real miracle was when Jonah returned home and told Mrs. Jonah where he was over the weekend. And she bought the story!

Well, it could have happened that way, although I am not sure if Jonah was ever married. The fact remains, there are great lessons to be learned from this Biblical story of Jonah. He experienced the unlimited mercy of God. Jonah, himself, who was not really convinced he had done any good, waited outside the city to see if God was going to spare it or not. He was certainly not a positive thinker.

Because of the intense hot weather at the time, Jonah built himself a makeshift shelter to get away from the blazing sun and heat. God, in his mercy, caused a large plant, a gourd, to grow overnight with big leaves to shelter him from the elements. Jonah appreciated it very much. The following night, God sent a worm to eat at the plant causing it to die. The leaves wilted and no longer provided shade for Jonah. He felt sorry for himself and for the plant. He was angry and wanted to die.

God had to remind and teach Jonah another lesson. Jonah had no pity on Nineveh, but he pitied the plant which he had nothing to do with. He didn't cause it to grow. God, on the other hand, called the people of Nineveh His own. He even had compassion on the cattle and other livestock in the town. Jonah thought he deserved to be angry that the gourd died and didn't give him shelter any longer, but he failed to see the benefits when an entire city is spared. He thought more of a plant than he did of God's people. God proved it was better to be merciful than angry. This is a point we must remember in times when we may tend to let "our anger kindle" when we should be merciful. I think that the prophet Micah says it best when he proclaims, *"He has showed you O man, what is good, and what does the Lord require of you but to do justice, and to love kindness, and to walk humbly with your God!"* (Micah 6:8, RSV).

In the remainder of the Old Testament, we find at least another half of a dozen prophets who preached to the nation of Israel trying to get them to repent and return to the Lord. The Israelites would historically repent, fall and go back to the wickedness in the eyes of the Lord. Zephaniah called the entire nation to repentance. "Come together and hold assembly, O shameless nation, before you are driven away like the drifting chaff, before there come upon you the fierce anger of the Lord," he warns them.

Malachi predicted the coming of the Lord. A Messiah was on His way. The prophet Malachi even predicted the forerunner of Jesus who was none other than John the Baptist. "A man to prepare the way," he says. All that was left was for the children of Israel to wait and ponder their history, which wasn't all that good considering the many, many times they fell away form the Lord's pathway. He reminded the people that although they may think the Lord changes, "For I the Lord do not change," he states. It was up to them to change their ways or else "be consumed" he said. If they would look back and reflect on their past they would see that God never changes. He is faithful and just, unlike those who seem to change with the changing wind. They had left Him; God hadn't left them.

Malachi reminded them of their heritage and told them they must keep the statutes and ordinances that Moses gave them. The Ten Commandments were to be practiced then as they must be today. If we don't practice them, we will suffer the consequences. Our obedience to the law will not save us, however. Through our love for God we will not be able to help ourselves other than to do His will and obey His commandments. It's what we want to do! May the grace of our Lord Jesus Christ be with us all. Amen.

THE GOSPEL

In the New Testament of the Holy Bible, the authors of the 27 books, or letters in some cases, all relate to the last will and testament of our Lord. This is His gift to us so that we may have the truth and knowledge about the God we believe in. It is the most important gift anyone could have bequeathed us: this gift of eternal life.

The Old Testament was completed and like the entire Bible "was all written for our instruction," the Bible tells us. Now we have Jesus on the scene - God who became man and "dwelt among us," as the apostle John states in his first chapter. Jesus wanted us to become absolutely aware that He did not come to abolish the laws of the old testament but to "fulfill them." All the prophecies of that era would now be fulfilled. Once again, He would prove to us that He uses people just like us to accomplish His great works. He uses people who sin and those rare ones who appear to live a near perfect life but have what is called "inherited sin." "In sin did my mother conceive me," David of old wrote.

I have always found it interesting how God acquires His mighty works. That's why I named this book, "Then God." As you may have noted in prior chapters, when things looked hopeless, "Then God" did something about it. He perhaps raised up a mighty man of valor to defeat the enemies of God in the Old Testament. Or He brought up a man like Moses and hardened him like fine steel to become the world's greatest leader. Or He may have changed the course of events that led to more links in the chain of events being altered so His will could be done. In the New Testament, He did the same thing. Only now,

He is physically there to be seen by thousands of people.

To me, and to most people, God the Father in heaven, seemed to look down on His creation and once again, see how corrupt it has become and decided to send a Savior, Jesus. In the Old Testament, God would often see the pitiful sight and just destroy it like He did with Sodom and Gomorrah, two of the worst sin-filled cities. These were places where sins of man like homosexuality were out of control. God didn't like all the wickedness. As Paul writes to the Romans, *"God gave them up to dishonorable passions-dishonoring their bodies among themselves and because they did not acknowledge God because of their base minds and improper conduct"* (Romans 1).

Perhaps God could foresee the outcome of those people, knowing they would never change. Now, it appears as if He has hope, as if He is telling us, "I'm going to give them a Savior to give them a second chance." If they hear the Word and study the Word, perhaps they will change their hearts and repent and cease from doing whatever it is they do that is sinful.

He provides us with the Bible, a handbook for daily living. He inspired authors throughout the ages to write books about Him, inspiring us to come to the truth and knowledge of Him who made us. Then it's up to us. It's our choice, just like in the Garden of Eden where Adam and Eve first made their decision.

Some claim, and often use as an excuse, that the Bible is too difficult to understand; therefore, the reason they don't read it. Those individuals need to take a lesson from one of the followers of Jesus, Philip, who, via the instructions of an angel, was told to get on a road from Jerusalem that led to Gaza. He did as the angel told him. On the way, he discovered an Ethiopian eunuch. The eunuch was in charge of all the treasures of his Queen, Candace of Ethiopia. The Bible tells us in the eighth chapter of Acts that the eunuch was sitting along the road reading from the book of Isaiah.

Philip talked to him and asked him if he understood what he was reading. The answer was no, "How can I unless someone guides me?" he asked Philip and invited Philip to join him. Philip told him the Good News of Jesus Christ. The Ethiopian was converted and baptized immediately since there was water nearby. We can do the same. Ask for help from someone you respect and let them guide you. We hear nothing more about this eunuch but we do know "he went on his way rejoicing." He may have converted thousands in his homeland. It's very possible, just because someone was led by the Holy Spirit to minister to him. God works that way.

Throughout these final chapters, I hope to bring to light many more examples of how God sets things in motion to complete His mission. The greatest thing is, He isn't done yet! He has need of you and me to bring the whole plan to completion. May God grant that we are ready for the task.

JOHN THE BAPTIST

The great Apostle, Luke, records a story of the coming of a man referred to as "John the Baptist." A priest named Zechariah was married for a number of years to a woman named Elizabeth. She, like several other women in Scripture, was noted as being barren or childless. They were getting on in years and hope was gone of ever having a child, let alone a son. They had prayed for years but no child was born to them.

Then one day while Zechariah was burning incense at an altar, he was visited by an angel who announced to him that their prayer had been heard. They would have a son, and they were to name him John, proving once again that in God's time frame, when He is ready, and you're ready, prayers will be answered.

Zechariah was told by the angel that his son would never drink wine nor any strong drink, and he would be filled with the Holy Spirit, even in his mother's womb. John would have the power to persuade men to truth and knowledge of the Lord, and he would have the power of Elijah, the greatest of the prophets.

Once again, we witness doubt. This time it filled Zechariah. "I am an old man and my wife is advanced in years, how can this be?" he questioned the angel, Gabriel. Abraham and Sarah had also questioned the angel, Gabriel. As Abraham and Sarah had also questioned angels when they were told of the coming of their son, Zechariah was no different. He probably thought about the fact that it was scientifically impossible at their age. They forgot that with God, everything is possible.

Because of his doubt, the angel struck him dumb or unable to speak until after the child was born. Those around knew he had seen a vision, or something, but weren't sure what.

Elizabeth had a cousin named Mary, the blessed Virgin Mary, in fact. She was betrothed to a man named Joseph, a carpenter, of the house of David. The same angel, Gabriel, visited Mary. The angel informed Mary of a son she would bear. He was to be so great of an individual He would be the "Son of the Most High," the angel informed her. "His Kingdom would have no end."

Mary was struck in wonderment, being a virgin, not yet married. "How was this to be?" she thought. But she refused to ponder on the "why" and stated, "Let it be according to thy word." She hurried to tell her cousin, Elizabeth, the good news. Upon entering the house, it is written the baby that Elizabeth was carrying, now about six months along, "leaped in her womb." The yet unborn John knew what was taking place.

It is believed that John was born a few months before Christ. He spent his early years in seclusion near his home in the hill country of Judah. Like Elijah, he lived like a hermit, dressed in camel skins, wore a leather girdle around his waist and lived on locusts and wild honey. He looked like a wild man. He was an individual that, if we met him today, we would not be excited to see him. We would, no doubt, "pre-judge" this man as one that we didn't need to become acquainted with.

Around A.D. 26, John began his preaching. He was a powerful preacher. He could convince his listeners they needed salvation and that they needed to repent. He was one of the first evangelists, I would say, who truly had a tremendous impact on the way preaching is performed by conservative preachers today.   He was a "voice crying in the wilderness, preparing the way of the Lord.   Make His paths straight," he shouted from his pulpit, which happened to be wherever he stood.   He laid it on those who "thought" they were living the way of the Lord.   John referred to them as a "brood of vipers," when these so-called "devout Jews" of the day would come to hear his preaching and criticize him.   He warned them, and all his listeners, that One was coming who was greater yet than he, One whose sandals he was too unworthy to even untie, as we read in Luke 3:16.

Then the One he spoke of did come.   Jesus was on his way to be baptized by John.   John knew the parents of Jesus.   It could be they played together when they were little boys, but most of all John was acquainted with Jesus' heavenly Father.   He felt unworthy saying "it is You who needs to baptize me," but Jesus did not want that.   Jesus convinced him that this is how it had to be, and John performed the act.   Immediately when Jesus came up from out of the water, the heavens opened and the Spirit of God descended from above and lighted on Him and a voice from the heavens declared, "This is My beloved Son with Whom I am well pleased!"   It was the Voice of God Himself.

Jesus was now ready for the ministry He was put on the this earth to conduct.   John, on the other hand, was finished.   As he stated, "He (meaning Jesus) must increase, I must decrease."   John had been the forerunner of Jesus.   The man who introduced Him to the public was done with his task.

John didn't care what the public felt about his way of preaching. He called the proverbial "spade, a spade" even when it meant his life would be in danger. He never pulled any punches. He called it like it was. If someone needed correcting, he did it with no fear. When he saw King Herod was living in sin with his brother's wife, Herodia, he admonished him. That got him thrown into prison. Later, on Herod's birthday, Herodia's daughter danced for him. King Herod told her that he would give her anything she wanted upon the occasion. Prompted by her mother, she said, "Give me the head of John the Baptist!" In order to make himself look like he was a man of his word in front of his friends, he regretfully had the request fulfilled. Herodia's daughter danced around the room with John's humble head on a platter, his blood dripping on the floor.

John's ministry was brief, perhaps only about one year, but his message has endured to this day. He will never "go away" as many wanted him to. Many historians agree that the fall of Herod's army in the war with Aretas soon after John's death may have been a divine judgement call for his beheading of this great individual, John the Baptist. John was unlike the other prophets who were only able to foretell of Christ's coming. John was able to point Him out.

JESUS, WHO IS CALLED CHRIST

It has been my intention in this book to write about those characters of Scripture who had a taste of sin, so to speak. They were like us, who were weak and easily overcome by temptations of this world, who sometimes fall hard. It's always interesting to see how God brings these people up again. They are often put to their knees where they must humble themselves to a gracious God for help.

Although there are several individuals in the Bible which we can find little or no fault in, they were all, nevertheless, humans, like you and I. There may not be anything written about the mistakes they may or may not have made, but be assured they sinned. They all lived with an inherited sin, the Bible teaches.

Even though we read of people like Enoch who "walked with God" all his life, and even John the Baptist as you read about in the prior chapter, it is written they were "righteous" individuals. John's parents "were both righteous", but we find where Zechariah doubted what was going to unfold for them with reference to the birth of John. He was not perfect either, or he would have never questioned what the angel told him.

One man in the entire Bible stands out. His name is Jesus, who is called the Christ. Jesus was His given name by the angel who visited Mary. That's what His name would be. "For He shall save His people form their sins," it reads. The name Christ comes from the anointed one, corresponding to the Hebrew word Messiah. In the old Testament we read of numerous times when prophets referred to the coming of the Messiah. Now He is born and lives forever!

As soon as Jesus was born, the world was never the same. No individual in the entire Bible has more of an impact on the world today as this man Jesus. No investigation of any person in history was more intense than it was, and is, of Jesus.

They still want to "follow" Him. He, who gave us the blueprints of life, is still being sought after today. We talk to Him in our prayers, and we see Him all around us. All we need to do is look. "Seek, and ye shall find," the Scriptures tell us.

The way in which He was born is one of the "stumbling blocks" of those who seem to want to believe but are unable to. In this highly educated world there are those who find it impossible to believe the ""virgin birth." They cannot comprehend a child "conceived by the Holy Spirit." Unless one has the faith of a little child, perhaps they never will. Nevertheless, the angel told Mary that it would happen that way, and it did. God's messenger is not to be argued with. It was at a point and time in history when God would fulfill what He had promised for thousands of years. It was the time that a Savior would be born to save His people from their sins. It was as if God's great time clock was finally reaching the hour when Scripture was to be fulfilled.

With all this talk about a Savior, people in those days thought He would be some great warrior that would come down from heaven and destroy all their enemies, and God's people would live happily ever after. Not so, even though this was what they wanted. But this was not a man that would directly save their mortal bodies from destruction. He would save their souls from everlasting death. He gave them a chance to "live forever." As John says concerning the people of God, *"So they would not perish but have everlasting life"* (John 3:16).

Here is a Child born to a virgin who was fearful herself. In those days, if a woman was to have a child with no husband, chances were she would be stoned to death. However, God was preparing sort of a step-father for Jesus His name was Joseph, a local carpenter, and he would be the Child's father. He would marry this woman, help her raise this Child and bring Him up in the ways of the Lord. They were not princely people, not rich in wealth, but they were rich in love and filled with the love of God. They had all the qualifications of good parents, and the Lord was well aware of that. They were a perfect couple to raise His Son.

I think it was Albert Einstein who made the statement one time like this, "I want to know God's Father." The inquisitive mind of this great individual who knew the answer to splitting the atom was overwhelmed by the Trinity of God: the Father, Son and Holy Spirit. Einstein even searched for the answers to the mysteries of God. With all the intellect he was gifted with, Einstein was aware that God did exist.

Jesus was born in a lowly stable one night in Bethlehem. The local hotels were filled up because everyone was going to their respective cities and towns of their lineage to be enrolled. This was like being registered in a census because Caesar Augustus wanted a count of the population. This strategy is still used to this day to determine the numbers so in times of wars, the leaders of the country can know how many people they could count on both for support and nonsupport. It also gave them the information on how much tax can be collected which was also important to them.

So it was in this environment that Jesus was born. Shepherds in the hills were told of it by God's Holy angels. Wise men followed a star to the cradle searching for Him. We, today, still search for Him in some way or another.

King Herod searched for Him, too. Word had reached his throne about a new "King of the Jews," and he couldn't tolerate that. The King wanted to kill Jesus, this new threat to his kingdom. He sent his staff looking for the child, but the parents of Jesus, being warned by an angel, managed to keep one step ahead of them. They fled to Egypt, but Herod in his anger, failing to find Jesus, issued an order for all male babies under two years of age that lived around Bethlehem, to be killed. His order was carried out, but Jesus escaped. When Herod died, Jesus and His parents went back to the land of Israel.

The custom in those days was that each year the Jews would go to Jerusalem for Passover festivities. Jesus and His parents went, too. When Mary and Joseph were done at the festivities, they left for home along with this multitude of people. They noticed that Jesus wasn't by their side. He was twelve years old at the time and they assumed He was with some of the other relatives and continued their journey for one day. When they finally stopped to rest, they couldn't find the lad and like most parents, they became concerned. He was not with any of the family, so He must have stayed in Jerusalem. They hurried back and found their Son still standing in the temple listening to the teachers and asking questions.

They quickly admonished their Son, asking Him why He gave them such a worry because they had been frantic looking for Him. Jesus answered, *"How is I that you sought me? Did you not know that I must be in my Father's house?"* (Luke 2:49 RSV). Jesus was obedient and went with His parents, even though they did not understand what He meant. However, Mary, His mother, "kept all these things in her heart."

We don't read much of the life of Jesus again until he is around 30 years old when John baptizes Him. It is recorded that one time Jesus went up to a high mountain to be tempted by Satan who offered Him the world if He would only bow down and worship this "king of sin". Jesus rebuked the Devil. The Devil left Jesus, knowing he would not persuade this "Son of God."

Jesus went on to teach, preach and heal. He made His Presence known. He made a terrific impact, gaining followers to carry on His work throughout the centuries. He stunned the so-called "religious leaders" of that day with His knowledge and like most of those who think they are wise, they rejected Him. The religious leaders plotted to kill Him, the One who had the power to save them from their sins. Jesus pronounced many "woes" unto them, warning them of their failure to see the way of the truth and the life. This made them even more angry and their tempers towards Him caused them to conspire even more to have Him killed. Jesus gave the people many prophecies that His enemies didn't like to hear either. Being totally confounded by this man Jesus, they paid one of His followers, Judas Iscariot, to betray Him. Judas was paid to point Jesus out with a kiss so to properly identify the Man that was causing all the revolt in town. Judas did, and Jesus was arrested.

Through this kangaroo court of a trial, all the evidence was brought out concerning Jesus by the lawyers, scribes and high priests. When the trial was nearly over, even Pontius Pilate, a Roman procurator at the time, who had the power to judge Jesus, even he, while washing his hand in a pan, stated, "I find no crime in this man."

The people against Jesus wanted justice, so they had Pilate send Jesus to Herod, in the higher court. Herod happened to be in Jerusalem at the time. Because Jerusalem was in his jurisdiction, he could make the call. He questioned Jesus, but Jesus would not answer him. The people continued to mock Him, saying He was the King of the Jews. Herod sent Him back to Pilate. Pilate didn't want the blood of this innocent Man on his hands, so he let the people decide. He even went so far as to bring out another prisoner by the name of Barabbas, a murderer, letting the people choose who they wanted the most to be put to death, Jesus or Barabbas. They chose Jesus, and Pilate and Herod let Jesus be convicted.

Up on a hill where the sentence was to be carried out, they crucified Jesus along with two other criminals, one at His right and one at His left. The soldiers nailed His feet and hands upon a wooden cross and waited for Him to die. One convict asked Jesus to save Himself and them if He really was the Son of God. The other stated that although the convicts deserved to die, Jesus did not. This convict asked Jesus to remember him when He entered into His Kingdom. Jesus answered him, "Truly I say unto you, today you will be with me in Paradise."

The story of the penitent thief would go down in history to proclaim that even at the last moment of life, one can be saved if they repent. Jesus had referred to this earlier in His preaching when He spoke of the laborers in the vineyard. He told how workers at the beginning of the day agreed to be paid one denarius to work in the vineyard all day. Some of the workers came in later and later yet and at the end of the day they were all paid the same, one denarius. Those who had worked a full day grumbled because the one who had only worked for an hour got paid the same as they. It didn't seem fair. Jesus asked them quoting the landowner who paid them, "Do you begrudge my generosity? Am I not allowed to do as I choose with what belongs to me?" Then the profound statement, "So the last will be first and the first, last!"

Those who repent at the last moment will be saved is the bottom line. Those who have practiced their faith all their lives are blessed with the fruits of it. How much of a greater life one has when he or she is a practicing Christian! I would believe that the thief on the cross would have loved to have served the Lord all his life rather than to do what he did, like, "running from the law" as we would refer to it today. The reward will be the same, Jesus said. It all depends on when one repents and comes to Christ that makes all the difference in our next life.

I truly believe the thief who repented died happier than the betrayer, Judas Iscariot. Although he, too, noted his error in sending an innocent man, Jesus, to his death in Matthew 22, he even gave back the thirty pieces of silver he was paid to betray Jesus. He told the chief priests, "I have sinned," to which they responded, "What is that to us?" Judas then ran out of the building and hanged himself. He couldn't live with it. He took his own life and compounded the sin he was already burdened with. Some liberal-thinking Christians who stand firm think Judas is in heaven. Although I cannot judge the man, the Bible teaches that it is highly improbable that he is in heaven.

The question for us is one that Pilate posed when he asked the people "Then what shall I do with Jesus who is called the Christ?" What are YOU going to do with Jesus is the question. Will you believe in Him or reject Him? It has to be one or the other. With Christ there is not much compromise. Jesus said, "You cannot serve two masters. You will either love one and hate the other." My prayer is that you choose to serve Jesus who is called the Christ.

NICODEMUS

Everyone knew that the Pharisees disliked Jesus. Jesus had made them more hateful of Him when He rebuked them. People don't like it when someone tells them they are wrong. He addressed them for what they were, a bunch of guys who thought they knew religion better than He did. However, one man, seeing all the miracles Jesus performed, wondered about this man, Jesus. Nicodemus tended to believe what he had seen and wanted to know more. The Holy Spirit had touched him.

We note in John 3, that Nicodemus came to Jesus by night. Far be it that his colleagues and fellow rulers of the Jews would see him conversing with Jesus, whom they all despised. Or Nicodemus may have had a sincere motive of wanting to visit with Jesus privately, perhaps as a form of counseling. Nicodemus admitted to Jesus that he believed that Jesus "comes from God."

Recognizing that Jesus did indeed have some relationship with God, Nicodemus was willing to learn. Jesus, who of course knew why Nicodemus was there, asked him a question which would confound most any individual and still does today. "Truly I say to you, unless one is born anew, he cannot see the kingdom of God."

Nicodemus was confused, thinking that he must again be born out of his mother's womb, but Jesus quickly set His message straight. He must be born of water and the Spirit. He elaborated by saying, "the wind blows where it will, and you hear the sound of it, but you do not know whence it comes or whither it goes, so it is with everyone who is born of the Spirit."

His student still didn't understand this statement and Jesus reminded him that he was a teacher of Israel. Why didn't he understand this? "Why, what kind of teacher are you," He asks. Jesus continued to reprimand him by telling him that he failed to believe earthly things, so how could he believe the heavenly things Jesus informed him of.

The Spirit is an essential element in our lives. Jesus refers to it being "like the wind." You can't see the Spirit but can hear it. Do you "hear" the Spirit? Jesus is saying to us, as well as to Nicodemus, that we must hear. Some believe it comes in a form of conscience, while others believe it is a gift direct from God. However you "hear" it doesn't matter, as long as you know it is from God. Listen. God talks to you in some way or another. I know, I've heard Him.

Nicodemus was like many who wonder if Jesus is real. They are almost convinced but "knowledge" keeps them from totally and completely accepting Jesus as their Savior. Nicodemus couldn't understand what it meant to be "born again," nor could he comprehend, at least at that time, being born of water and the Spirit. Being baptized and receiving the Holy Spirit was something he had not studied. He knew the Jews must be circumcised, had studied the laws given by Moses and he thought he had it made. That was not the case here, or anywhere else, and Jesus tried to tell him what he needed.

Later on, it would appear that Nicodemus tried to defend Jesus at a private meeting the chief priests and the Pharisees had concerning Jesus. Nicodemus stated, "Does our law judge a man without first giving him a hearing and learning what he does?" They asked Jesus if He was from Galilee, too, for they thought that no prophet was ever to rise out of Galilee. The council assumed Jesus was from Galilee, which was false. They were just not willing to hear Nicodemus because he was throwing their laws back in their faces, and they became confused. They adjourned the meeting and went stomping home.

No, these Pharisees did not want to "listen" to Jesus and learn more about Him. Nicodemus was in a group of peers which probably was highly uncomfortable for him at this time because he was touched by the Spirit even though he didn't know it. Jesus had informed Nicodemus that he must accept Him by faith and not by works of the law. I think Nicodemus believed it.

He proved his respect for Jesus when Joseph of Arimathea asked Pilate for the body of Jesus and it was give to him. Nicodemus brought one hundred pounds of myrrh and aloes, precious spices mixed together, to preserve the body. He helped wrap Jesus in linens and laid Him in a tomb, not knowing that in three days He would rise again, assuring us that we, too, when we die, will have the same opportunity.

We don't know what became of this Jew named Nicodemus, the man who embalmed Jesus. He, no doubt, heard about the resurrection and I imagine he believed it. We saw no outward conversion of him like we do with others we will explore in later chapters, but everyone does not come to Christ in the same manner. The important thing is that Nicodemus literally came to Christ, even though it was at night. Christ does not care when or where we come to Him. The important thing is that you and I accept Him as our Savior.

No matter what condition we are in, we must come. An old-time bar maid wrote a hymn and in it, she states, "Just as I am without one plea. But that thy blood was shed for me, and that thou bidst me come to thee, O lamb of God, I come, I come."

ZACCHAEUS

I can say, with all certainty, that many different individuals were brought to the truth and knowledge of Jesus Christ during the time of our Savior. Many were probably not mentioned in Scripture, but some are. Perhaps the recorder at the time, Luke, saw something special about the man, Zacchaeus. Luke refers to him as being a "chief tax collector." He was also very rich. He was a hated man by many. Some were jealous, some envious, some thought he was a crook and just wandered around taking their money via taxation. The more he collected, the more per cent he could keep for himself.

Recently, I watched and listened to a Sunday School program based on this story of Zacchaeus. I have heard many, many sermons using him as an example for us. He was often refereed to as "chief of sinners," which compounded his image. Perhaps he was, and that is why Jesus proclaims at the end of the story that He has come to seek and to save the lost. Zacchaeus, according to Jesus, was a lost man and became an example for us.

This little Jewish man was curious about Jesus. Perhaps he had heard of Him and wanted to know more about Him. He wanted to "see Jesus" which is in itself an admirable quality in any individual. I would want to see Jesus if I knew He was coming to my area. I certainly hope to see Jesus when I die, and I am assured that I will.

Zacchaeus was not blessed with height and could not peer over the heads of the crowds. Instead, he chose to run ahead of everyone and climb up a sycamore tree which was along the path that he was sure that Jesus would take. There he waited, peering through the dust the crowds stirred up, looking for the Man who had performed miracles like healing a blind man just shortly before He entered the streets of Jericho. Like a little boy, Zacchaeus had climbed the tree. Perhaps this was the key to his salvation, for Jesus said, "Unless you become as a little child you cannot enter into heaven." Zacchaeus, unknowingly, had begun to act like that child.

Well, Jesus did see him up in that tree and looked up at him and said, "Zacchaeus, make haste and come down for I must stay at your house today!" Oh, oh. Did Jesus make a mistake here by inviting Himself to the house of a man that everyone knew was a sinner? No, He did not, for this was the mission of Jesus: to seek and to save the lost. But His adversaries were quick to point out this fact when He stood trial later in His life - He associated Himself with people like Zacchaeus. Those people who thought they were "saints," would refuse to have anything to do with those who were known to sin. At some point in their lives, they had been taught that they should avoid those kinds of people for fear of their sin rubbing off. Some would call it peer pressure, or perhaps the fear of believing what sinners do is okay would be another excuse. Jesus taught us to not shun the sinner, the lost one, but bring him or her back into the fold. We have been shown that instead of standing away from those known sinners and then talking behind their backs, we are to confront them and bring them to Jesus.

Zacchaeus was different than most. He knew he was sinner and apparently in need of a Savior. The Holy Spirit had convicted him before he came to

Jesus. He acknowledged the fact that "if" he had ever defrauded anyone he would restore it fourfold. He even went so far as to tell Jesus that he would be willing to give half his assets to the poor. Perhaps he knew that he indeed had not always been charitable to the poor and actually had cheated people. He was performing the act of repentance. Jesus was well aware of his background, and Zacchaeus was, indeed, ready to receive Christ as his Lord and Master. Zacchaeus would shame many of us.

When the Lord told him to "make haste," Zacchaeus did not want to wait a second longer to receive this great blessing that Jesus had bestowed on him. Jesus called him by his name, the same as He does with us. He knew Zacchaeus, and He was aware of his needs, like He is aware of ours. As the hymn writer declares, "Why do we tarry when Jesus is calling?" Zacchaeus didn't tarry but scrambled down and let Jesus come to his house and into his heart.

"Today salvation has come to your house," Jesus told Zacchaeus. Wow! Jesus said this not only to Zacchaeus, but his entire household. The statement shows us that wherever Jesus comes, salvation does, too. How wonderful this good news is. Behold, Jesus stands at your door and knocks! Will you let Him in, or ignore the knock?

You may be a young person with a family with little toddlers running around the house. Letting Jesus in your life can mean salvation for all of you, He teaches us. Children unexposed to the Savior will be like orphans and lost sheep later on in life. They will have no leader, no shepherd. While they are home, they have parents to be a role model, and with Jesus in your life you will not let them down.

Or you may be an older person, a senior citizen with grown children, or perhaps you are even childless. You can be a role model with Christ in your life. You may be surrounded by people, or you may be a lonely person, but there will be a time when someone will see your "works," as Jesus did with Zacchaeus, and proclaim that you know Jesus. It may be in a nursing home or on a hospital bed, but there will be those who will see Jesus through you. You may turn out to be an inspiration to them.

I recall one lady, Anna, who was in a nursing home. Several members of the staff of nurses did not know Jesus. They had not, at the time, answered the door when Jesus knocked. Anna would sit by her desk daily in her little room and read the Bible though she had failing eyesight. Nurses would come in and out of her room and witness this and wonder how she could think of Jesus when her health was failing so fast due to a painful form of cancer. The nurses would comment that if Jesus was so real to her, why did she have to suffer so much? They had watched many patients face death who did not know Jesus and cursed Him on their deathbeds. What made Anna different?

For Anna it was not suffering as some of the nurses would have labeled it. By reading her Bible, she got better acquainted with the One who would soon take her home. For Anna it was a time of rejoicing, because she knew that soon she would truly see Jesus. All the pain and suffering would soon be gone, and she would meet Jesus face to face, much like Zacchaeus. Her sins were washed away and forgiven, and soon she would enter into the house of Jesus. He had lived with her. Now, when

she closed her eyes in death, she would live with Him
eternally.

THE TWELVE

There were twelve of them: men who were called disciples, or those who Isaiah referred to as "those who are taught of God." Disciples are defined as those who are pupils or followers of a public teacher, like John the Baptist. Those students who received instruction from the Divine Master are truly called disciples. These men were conducting their everyday business, and "Then God" stepped in and changed their lives.

These particular twelve men were also referred to as apostles – men who were sent on a mission to proclaim the works of Jesus – men who witnessed His life.

Paul is often referred to as an apostle but humbly refers to himself as "the least of the apostles." Paul stated he had persecuted the church in his early years and was unfit to be called an apostle, even though he was divinely chosen. He had seen Jesus after the resurrection, but he still felt that he wasn't qualified to have been bestowed this high honor.

Although Paul was not one of the twelve chosen in the beginning of the life of Jesus, we will see in a later chapter the very important role he fulfilled in spreading the gospel.

The first twelve men were not popular guys. The fact is the Jews thought they were illiterate. They were simple men, not highly educated, and for the most part they were simple fishermen. Today, many are chosen or appointed by a governor or President of the United States who are men and women of great knowledge, popularity, political savvy or people who would serve their leader in such a beneficial way so that they would have no problem in getting elected the next term.

Jesus didn't choose people like that, but they met His qualifications nonetheless. They were to be ambassadors to His divine purpose of spreading the Gospel to all nations. They were to be the beginning of something very big. They were even unaware of the magnitude of their mission. These twelve humble men, as if they were to be in a great courtroom involving the whole world, were to testify on the behalf of Jesus. This was a mission so big that if they were to have known, they probably would not have accepted the job.

In most instances, these simple men of faith accepted what Jesus told them without question. They believed in Him because they had heard and had seen Him. Unlike those who, as Jesus said, "believe and have not seen," who are called "blessed," these men of old were truly able to testify as to what they had seen and Who Jesus was. Their mission was to convince those who had not had the privilege of actually living with this Man called Jesus Christ. Their job was to persuade people throughout the ages that Jesus was definitely real – a task that many fail to accomplish to this very day.

These men were the chosen twelve that Jesus called and were more than likely called in this order: Simon Peter and his brother Andrew; James and John, the sons of Zebedee; Philip; Nathanael, who is also named Bartholomew; Matthew, who is also called Levi; Thomas; James, the son of Alphaeus; Thaddaeus, or Judas, the son of James; Simon, the Zealot from Canaan; Judas Iscariot.

God's plan was to have as many apostles as there were tribes of Israel, which was twelve. When

Judas Iscariot hanged himself after he betrayed Jesus, there was a need to elect another apostle. Two men who qualified for the position, Joseph, also called Barrabas, and Matthias, were voted upon by the rest of the Apostles to fill the vacancy. Matthias was elected.

I think it's beneficial to look at each of these individuals more closely to perhaps get an insight as to why Jesus chose them. It may be significant to us, and why He chooses us to that high calling of being disciples.

I am always amused at those who say they "have nothing to do." The job of being a disciple is never-ending, and there is always plenty to be done. No one should have the excuse of being bored. This is the highest calling one can have, and rest assured, you are being called. The only criterion is for you to say, "YES!"

These twelve men all had jobs, but they walked away from them and followed Jesus. They lived only on what they had or had been given to them. In this age of people needing or wanting to be "secure" in what they do, a disciple of Christ does not busy himself with being anxious about tomorrow, but he lives for today with the hope of a great tomorrow and eternal life.

In the life of Jesus, it seemed to happen like this: One day, Jesus was walking by the Sea of Galilee and saw a couple of guys fishing with nets in a boat. It was Peter and Andrew. Jesus shouted at them saying, "Follow Me and I will make you fishers of men!" They left their nets and followed Him, just as simple as that.

PETER, THE ROCK

It is believed that Peter was probably a disciple of John the Baptist. It was Andrew, his brother, who introduced him to Jesus (John 1: 41-42). Jesus immediately renamed him, Cephas, which means Peter, which means the "Rock."

Peter was to abide with Jesus in three ways: first, as a disciple; second, as His constant companion; and third, as an apostle as is recorded in Scripture. Peter is depicted as being the most bold, rough and possibly the largest disciple. He was not intimidated by anyone because of his character.

His life, much like the lives of our own, is marked in three stages. The first was a period of training where he learned about Christ and himself. It is important to note that to know Christ, you must also know yourself. Who are you? Are you fit for the kingdom? Many questions can enter a person's mind when one associates their life with Christ.

During his second stage, he underwent a period of leadership within the church. When we get to know Christ and join a church, we often become a leader of that church. That is what we yearn to do when we are Christ's disciples.

The third period was a time of humble work for the sake of Christ. He became a preacher, as we see in the book of Acts which lists his first sermon. He wrote two epistles that further explain his devotion to the Lord. Again, like many of us, we get to know the Lord and cannot keep still about it. We preach, and often write to further proclaim the Gospel of Jesus Christ. This is humble work, usually not met with much honor to those around us, but knowing that we honor the Lord is gratification enough. This is what Peter did.

But this bold man fell, too, the same way that we do. When Jesus was depending on his disciples to watch and pray in the garden, Peter was one of those who fell asleep. When Jesus needed him the most to testify for Him, Peter denied that he knew Jesus not only once but three times. He was afraid for his life. He wept over it later and expressed his sorrow as an example to us that when we let Jesus down, we should have a repenting heart, too, and come back to Christ.

This man, Peter, who boasted to Jesus that he would never fall away from Him, did. He refused to accept the fact by saying that even if he were asked to die for Him that he would never deny Him. Jesus predicted that before the cock crowed, Peter would deny Him three times. He did. "The Rock" crumbled when people asked him if he knew Jesus. Three times he was asked if he knew Jesus, and three times he pretended he didn't. After the third time, the cock crowed, and Peter knew what he had done. He cracked when two maids of the courtyard and some bystanders accused him of knowing Jesus. The Bible tells us that Peter went out and wept bitterly. Knowing the wrong he had done perhaps made him more vigorous to spread the gospel. Often, guilt leads one to proclaim the truth even harder – such seemed to be the case of Peter.

But Jesus, who knows us better than we know ourselves, proclaimed to Peter in Matthew 16:18, that Peter would become the foundation of His church. *"Upon this Rock I will build my church,"* Jesus tells him. What an honor and great privilege for a man to have, knowing that around him the church would be built. The church is a rock that cannot be moved - one that the gates of hell itself shall never prevail against. Peter had a huge responsibility at the same time, and thought he was fit for the job. He seems to have boasted a little about his qualifications, but was shot down quickly by Jesus.

In the very next paragraph of Matthew 16 beginning with verse 21, Jesus told the disciples of events that were about to happen. Jesus told them of His death and resurrection that would occur three days later. It is Peter who quickly states, *"God forbid Lord, that this should ever happen to you."*

Unknowingly, he becomes like Satan to Jesus. Jesus says, *"Get thee behind me Satan. You are a hindrance to me, for you are not on the side of God but of men!"* Peter wanted to protect his Master. He thought he could control Jesus' destiny, but Jesus reminded him that it is God the Father who decides what was about to happen concerning Jesus. The prophecies had to be fulfilled, and Peter would need to learn that. Who are we to decide what God's will is? Peter didn't have the right, either. When the enemies of Jesus came to arrest Him, Peter took his sword and cut off the ear of one of the men that was going to take Jesus. Luke records the fact that Jesus reprimanded Peter again and touched the ear of the man and healed the ear.

Peter meant well by his actions even though they weren't always what God intended. He became one of the great men of the Scriptures, and his boldness is admired by many. He was indeed a preacher of the Gospel. He could heal people, as is noted many times in the Bible, and he could perform other miracles. He defended the church. He also knew what it was like to be in prison. He was a great man and is an example for us.

His humbleness is noted as well when he is put to death for proclaiming the Gospel, a commission he was destined to fulfill. He died a martyr's death by crucifixion for proclaiming the saving Gospel of Jesus Christ. Legend has it that even in his dying hour, Peter humbled himself to be crucified upside down as to not honor his body with being crucified in the same manner as Christ.

ANDREW

Like his brother Peter, Andrew was a fisherman. He was a commercial fisherman, evidently, because he and Peter were found using nets. This was not a hard trade to learn, but it was one of necessity. People had to eat and bought fish from these brothers.

Andrew was a disciple of John the Baptist, and John the Baptist had taught Andrew that Jesus was truly the Son of God. Andrew introduced Jesus to his brother, Peter. This is the way brothers and other family should conduct themselves. When one finds Jesus, they should not hesitate to introduce Him to other members of the family. The Bible teaches that when one is "saved," they are not the only one who has discovered salvation, but their whole household. They should convert the rest of the family by their good works. However, some members of the family may reject Christ, the Son of the living God, due to the hardness of their hearts.

On one occasion, Jesus was preaching His gospel to five thousand people. It was Andrew who told Jesus of the lad that had five loaves of bread and two fishes. Jesus converted that small amount of food into enough to feed all five thousand present at that event. So much food was created that they had twelve baskets of leftovers to collect "so nothing was lost" Jesus said. Jesus didn't believe in throwing good food away.

We aren't told much about the life of Andrew other than the fact that he was a devout follower of Jesus. He was another one of the apostles and a permanent one. When the choice is made to follow

Jesus, it should be just as permanent for us as it was for Andrew.

According to historians, Andrew also died a martyr's death. He requested to be crucified on a cross in the form of an "X." In his humility, he probably didn't think he deserved the honor of being put to death in the same form as Christ either, like his brother, Peter, believed. The cross is known today as "St. Andrew's Cross." There is also a bay in Scotland named St. Andrew's Bay. He became the patron saint of Scotland because mariners who brought the gospel there bore two relics of Andrew with them that were later found in a wrecked ship. Both Greek and Roman churches celebrate a festival on the 30th of November each year in honor of St. Andrew. A town in Scotland is named in his honor. In the Church of England on that day, a sermon in preached on mission work with Andrew in mind. It has been said that he preached from his cross until he closed his eyes in death.

What a guy he must have been. Here again we see how when Jesus met a lowly fisherman, "Then God" made him a mighty Christian. He can do the same with us.

JAMES & JOHN

These two sons of Zebedee were different from Peter and Andrew. Scriptures tell us that they must have been some of the most trusted of all the twelve disciples. James had the distinct honor to be present, along with John and Peter, at the mount of transfiguration when Moses and Elijah appeared before Jesus.

James and John were partners with Peter and Andrew as fishermen. Both James and John were with their father fishing in a boat when Jesus called them to follow Him. One must note the fact that they left their boat "immediately," leaving their father alone in the boat. As far as we know, they never looked back but kept their eyes focused on Jesus.

It is also possible, and is assumed, that because their mother is referred to as Salome, she would have been a sister to Mary, the mother of Jesus, making them a relative to Him. No wonder Jesus seemed to be fond of the two.

Jesus also rebuked James and John upon occasion. Jesus was traveling to Jerusalem by way of a Samaritan village. Messengers were sent ahead to prepare for the arrival of Jesus. They would not accept Him at that time. They were at a verbal war with Jerusalem, and the two towns had no use for each other. They would not accept Jesus because he was heading towards Jerusalem. Samaritans wanted Jesus' place of worship to be at Mount Girizim in their own land. The two tribes of Jews and Gentiles hated one another because of jealousy. Little did they know that the place of worship would neither be in Jerusalem nor on this mountain in Samaria.

When James and John heard about the refusal of the Samaritans to accept Jesus, they suggested that Jesus allow them to bid fire to come down from heaven and wipe their people out. But Jesus said, "No," and went on to another village instead. Getting even with people was not Jesus' way, nor should it be ours. He taught them to ignore some of the things that bothered them and stressed love and kindness to all people.

On another occasion, both James and John proved to Jesus that they were overly ambitious people. They were glory seekers, an attribute Jesus didn't care for. They had the nerve to tell Jesus that He should give them what they wanted, which was that He should allow them to sit next to Him, one on His left and the other on His right, when He returned to heaven. Jesus simply told them that their wish was not His to grant. The other ten apostles didn't appreciate the request of James and John either. The two had seen the popularity of their Master and wanted to elevate themselves to His height, which for sure would not be possible.

They, no doubt, were taught the error of their ways by Jesus and went on to be fine disciples of His. Their defects in character were overcome, and they both became elements of strength and glory in the time to come.

John was known for his deep spiritual insight and loving disposition, and Jesus loved that. Unlike Peter, he followed Jesus to His very death on the cross. From the cross, Jesus entrusted the care of His mother to John. He knew He could trust that John would take good care of her.

After Pentecost, John became a colleague of Peter, being busy in missionary work. He also knew what it was to be imprisoned for the sake of the Gospel for a short time. He wrote the Gospel of John, three epistles and the book of Revelation. He was a pillar of strength for Paul when the work of the early church was in its beginnings.

James died a martyr's death by the hand of Herod with a sword, the first of this apostolic band to seal his testimony with his blood. John, on the other hand, lived to a ripe old age, dying of natural causes as best we know. John, it is believed, was the only one of the apostles who did not die a martyr's death, although his enemies tried to kill him on at least one occasion. He was placed in a cauldron of boiling oil, an atrocious act that would have killed most people just by shock alone. John miraculously survived.

He was then banished to the Isle of Patmos where he died at a ripe old age.

PHILIP & NATHANAEL

While in Galilee, Jesus met Philip who was from the same town of Bethsaida where Andrew and Peter were from. Jesus simply said to him, "Follow me," and he did. With the invitation comes the call to be a disciple.

How nice it is to see that immediately following that he goes and finds Nathanael (John 1:45). He relates the news that he has found Jesus of whom the law spoke so much about – "Jesus of Nazareth." Little did Philip know that it was not he who found Nathanael, but Christ Himself. Many of us claim, "we have found Jesus," and boast about it, in a sense. It is never that way. It was Jesus who waits, seeking His people, and when the time is right, we finally accept him. "Jesus came to seek and to save," the Bible tells us. The question is, will we let ourselves be found?

Nathanael seemed to have a problem with Nazareth. Nathanael commented, "Can anything good come out of Nazareth?" History tells us that Nazareth did have a questionable reputation at times.

Nathanael's remark that good things never came out of Nazareth is thought provoking. It is possible that he was just using caution when he made this remark? People had been looking forward to the coming of Jesus for hundreds of years. Could He really be here now and from Nazareth? It appears that he was unaware that Jesus was from Nazareth and was ignorant of where Jesus was born. Philip, saying that Jesus was from Nazareth, caught Nathanael completely off guard.

Philip quickly invited him to "come and see." "Don't take my word for it, but look for yourself," he told Nathanael. Though convinced himself, he is unable to verbally convince Nathanael.

Jesus saw Nathanael coming and complimented him for being an Israelite, to which Nathanael answered, "How did you know me?" The response of Jesus had its impact on Nathanael when he heard his Lord say, "Before Philip called you, when you were under the fig tree, `I SAW YOU!'" Jesus took away the doubt of this true son of Jacob. Jesus verified for him that he was acceptable to Him, even before Nathanael had been introduced to Jesus.

That blew Nathanael's mind. He stated, "You are the Son of God!" He knew it was really Him. Jesus knew what only Nathanael knew: he had indeed been under a fig tree earlier. This is another point proven that God knows us before we know Him.

As for Nathanael, he hadn't seen anything yet! Jesus reminded him, "You shall see greater things than these!" And indeed he would. Nathanael, full of faith, had no idea what was in store for him and the other disciples.

At the feeding of the five thousand, it was Philip who was asked by Jesus as to how they were going to feed all the people. It was Philip who calculated it out, stating it would no doubt take two hundred denarii to buy enough bread for them all. One denarius was a day's wages in those days. It would have taken enough money that one man working for two hundred days would have to have in hand, and I doubt anyone had that much cash on hand. But Jesus had to show Philip a miracle. With the help of Andrew who had informed Jesus of five barley loaves of bread and two fishes a young boy had with him, He did show them a miracle. He fed five thousand people from the food the young boy brought and then when everyone had eaten, they gathered the leftovers so none would be wasted (John 6:1-14). No doubt, Philip stood in awe as he witnessed this great miracle.

Later, in John's Gospel, chapter 14, it is again Philip who still wondered about Who Jesus really is. Jesus was talking about His Father and Philip asked Him, "Show us the Father and we shall be satisfied." The statement disgusted Jesus. As long as they had known Him, they still did not understand that He and the Father were One. These disciples were truly Israelites. In the Old Testament, the Israelites were constantly wandering away from their Lord. They were full of doubts and fears within - often to the point of destruction. Now it is Philip who wants more. He's got Christ within arm's reach but still wonders and can't understand about the Holy Trinity, the three-in-one concept of the Holy Christian Faith.

The important thing about Philip is the fact that he remained true to Jesus. He is named in the book of Acts as the one being in the upper room to become another witness to the resurrection and after Jesus ascended into heaven. Not much more is known about him. It is believed Nathanael died by being flayed alive. Philip also died a martyr's death, but it is uncertain how. He died in Phrygia.

Nathanael, whom Jesus referred to as "in whom is no guile," is commendable. Nathanael was a good man, even though Jesus did remind him of his Israelite heritage of backsliders. He was not a crafty, sly or deceitful individual but proved to be a man of great faith. Nathanael also went by the name Bartholomew and is often referred to in Scriptures as one of the finest disciples. He was one of the disciples in the boat where they had been fishing all night and caught nothing. It was this, the third occasion, that Jesus revealed Himself to them. They were about one hundred yards from shore when Jesus shouted the question, "Caught anything?" When they answered grimly, "No," He told them to cast their nets on the other side of the boat. They did, and their nets were nearly busting at the seams, they had so many fish. They drug the net to shore where Jesus was waiting with a charcoal fire burning ready to fix breakfast for them. Nathanael, along with the rest, knew it was the Lord, and it is certain they were delighted to dine with their Lord.

THOMAS

If you have ever heard the old phrase, "Doubting Thomas," here is where it originated. He is known as the "doubter." Perhaps every group has to have one, and in this lot of twelve, he was it. I have seen this type of individual in practically every gathering of people I have ever been associated with. There always seems to be one who questions everything – the negative individual who wonders how this or that will ever succeed. He's often called a pessimist. Although Thomas wasn't all the above, he, nonetheless, was a doubter. He portrays a precise lesson for all of us.

Thomas had his admirable qualities, too, like most followers of Jesus. Once, when Jesus was planning on going back to Judea when He heard that His friend, Lazarus was ill, it was Thomas who argued with the rest of the disciples to accompany Jesus back to Judea. The rest were fearful that Jesus would be killed. He had been threatened on an earlier occasion when the Jews were about to stone Him. Thomas was ready to go along "so that we may die with Him." They all returned, and all went well, but Lazarus had already died. To show His love, Jesus restored Lazarus back to life.

On another occasion, Jesus was speaking of a place that He was going "to prepare a place" for them. Thomas didn't understand the meaning of that. He stated that he didn't know the way to get where Jesus was going. It was then that Jesus made one of His most powerful statements used widely to this day when he said, "I am the Way, the Truth and the Life!"

Thomas was not at the first meeting with the risen Lord. When he heard from some of the other disciples that Jesus had risen, he would not, and could not, believe it. "Unless I see in His hands the prints of the nails, and place my finger in the mark of the nails, and place my hand in His side, I will not believe!" That was that! He failed to believe the "hearsay" from his peers. He had to see for himself.

For eight days he probably pouted around about the matter while the other disciples still tried to convince him but failed. Perhaps wanting to believe, he could not, like so many of us today who doubt what we hear, even when we know the person or persons talking to us would never lie to us.

Then Jesus returned. He looked at Thomas and said go ahead and put your finger here, see my hands, put your hand in my side. Jesus told him, "Do not be faithless, but believing!" Thomas could only answer, "My Lord and my God!"

But Jesus wasn't finished with him yet. He told Thomas what is a great lesson for us when he stated, "Blessed are those who have not seen and yet believe."

It has been said of Thomas that he doubted so we might not doubt. Believe it. Jesus was, and is, real.

Thomas probably needed to do what he did. Perhaps it helped him to become one of the great missionaries later on in his life. It is noted in history that he went to India and preached and suffered death by martyrdom there when a lance pierced his body. A place near Madras is called St. Thomas Mountain after him.

Thomas is perhaps one of the greatest disciples who teaches us about the seriousness of having doubts, especially when it is about the Lord Jesus.

Want to be happy?   Jesus says again, "Happy (blessed) are those who believe and have not seen."

MATTHEW

When the Pharisee's condemned Jesus for keeping company with tax collectors, Matthew was the one who they were referring to. They looked upon this man as a sinner. He took their money, and history tells us that tax collectors probably took more than their share.

Looking at Jesus, I think much of His entire mission is reflected in this story about the call of Matthew. Recorded in Matthew 9, beginning with verse 9, we find Matthew sitting at his tax collection office. Jesus looked in and stated, "Follow me!" Immediately, Matthew arose and accepted the call.

Verse 10 says there were many other tax collectors and sinners sitting at the table with Matthew at his home. According to Luke, Matthew had prepared a big meal for his guests. Jesus was one of his guests. The Pharisees, seeing what was taking place, asked Jesus' disciples, "Why does your teacher eat with tax collectors and sinners?"

Jesus heard them mumbling and answered their question. "Those who are well are in no need of physician, but those who are sick. Go and learn what this means, I desire mercy, not sacrifice. For I came not to call the righteous but sinners!"

There you have it. The Pharisees thought they were very righteous doing what they thought the Law of Moses commanded them to do. They failed. Worse yet, they would not admit the fact that they, too, were sinners! At the same time, they would avoid those people who they thought were sinning. They thought that they knew more than anyone else. They were the "experts" in theology, and no one was going to tell them any different. Worse yet, they would have been delighted if a lightning bolt would have suddenly came down from heaven and struck Jesus dead. They wished the worst for Him Who was trying to educate them.

Jesus, knowing their hearts, tried to lead them in the right direction, but did they see what Jesus was doing? Apparently not, because they went ahead and crucified Him later. Very often, when people see or hear the truth, they still reject it. Their concern with wanting to be right and proud of it rewards them with death everlasting.

Matthew could have been one of them, but he chose to follow Christ. It is just another example of when Christ calls us, we are to make the decision to follow. Matthew went on to become one of the great apostles and preached to the Jews. He, no doubt, had some converts. He died a martyr's death via a sword in a distant city in Ethiopia. He died in Christ!

JAMES, THE LESS

Here is one disciple we know little about. We do know his mother was named Mary, he was one of the followers of Christ, and he had a brother called Joses or Barnabas according to Scripture (Mark 15:40). His father was Alphaeus.

It is speculated as to why he is referred to as "James the less," or the word "little" is sometimes used. Most scholars believe it was because of his size, being very small in stature. The other James was often referred to as "the greater," so when both were together, as they often were, they referred to them as such, thus distinguishing whom they were talking to.

When I think of an individual who is rather small in stature, I am reminded of one of the characters of the Old West. He may have been real or fictional, I'm not sure. They called him "Shorty" probably from the time he was old enough to walk. Bullies would push him around, and there was nothing he could do about it. He was too little to defend himself.

But Shorty grew older, and in those days of the 1800's, men still carried a sidearm. Shorty packed a short-barreled, bad 44-caliber revolver. He became very fast on the draw, practicing hour after hour on the farm where he lived. The gun, he felt, would make him a "bigger" man. In the story, it worked. Shorty no longer had to take the teasing he got because of his size, and when the first bully resented his challenge to "draw" the bully never lived to apologize. Shorty shot him dead.

As time went on, Shorty never meant to hurt anyone. He just wanted some respect. After a few of the local hotshots went to their graves, Shorty got respect, the story is told. He was known to tell those challenging him and addressing him as "Shorty" to "call him, `Mr. Shorty'" and they may live.

In those days the six gun was often an "equalizer," in such cases. Gang members still carry this concept of being the "big" man by the size of their gun. This is a very dangerous decision to make, first joining a gang and then trying to be the big man in it.

But in the case of James the Less, he was a mighty apostle. Back then, it took intestinal fortitude to be a follower of Christ and still does today. Many people then, and many today, have little respect for those who carry out the commission of our Lord Jesus Christ. It takes courage to become one of Jesus' followers. James had that courage. Later in his life, after witnessing countless sermons and confrontations Jesus had with all kinds of people, he continued carrying the Gospel as he had been told to do. But because of his size, those who hated him and his message easily manhandled him. They picked little James up, threw him out of a high and lofty opening in the temple where he landed in the street still alive – only to be clubbed to death by his enemies like some worthless dog. He died a martyr's death, like most of the apostles.

THADDAEUS, OR JUDAS, SON OF JAMES

Like a few other apostles, little is mentioned about this son of James. We know he was an apostle, and that's about it. Although it is not certain, some scholars consider Thaddaeus and Jude to be the same person. Not much historical data is available. He was indeed a "servant of the Lord Jesus Christ" as the book of Jude relates. He was also a brother of James, which makes it possible for these to be all one in the same.

He writes one of the shortest letters in the Bible, the book of Jude. However, it is a powerful one, packed with instructions for living, giving reference to those who do opposite the Lord's will as to "walk in the ways of Cain."

He talks as if he has gifted insight with respect to angels. Jude confirms that the angels will assist in executing the judgment on the day that Jesus comes again.

Until then, he reminds his readers that we are to practice our most Holy faith. "Pray in the Holy Spirit," he tells us. We are to convince those who doubt and save some by snatching them out of the fire, as he refers to sin.

He makes one think that we are, indeed, to be our brother's keeper. We are not to be concerned about our salvation alone but everyone else's, too. We are to treat our neighbors with tenderness and loving-kindness so that we, by any means possible, save some and bring them to salvation. This is a commission we all must observe.

Again, according to tradition and historical documents that have been found, Jude also died a martyr's death, being shot to death with arrows by his enemies, those who are probably residing in that place of everlasting torment – unless they repented.

SIMON, THE ZEALOT

Little is said of this Canaanite by the name of Simon. With two apostles carrying the same name, Simon the Zealot, or Canaanite, was used to distinguish him from Simon Peter.

We know Simon the Zealot was a member of the Jewish patriotic party; thus the title of "Zealot." The party began during the time of Cyrenius to resist Roman Oppression. Judas, the Galilean, appears to be the founder. In the end, the party was nothing more than a body of assassins called Sicarii.

We don't know if Simon was active in this type of party. He probably had an agenda until he met Jesus. Then it all changed. He would have no longer been set upon getting even with those that persecuted the Jews but would have turned the other cheek, as Jesus taught. Now he would be persecuted for his faith. According to historians, Simon the Zealot, also died a martyr's death. He died for Christ and in Christ.

JUDAS ISCARIOT

The last of the original twelve men who followed Jesus is Judas Iscariot. I have mentioned him in prior chapters as the betrayer of Christ. With one kiss he sold his Master out to the enemies of Jesus and His followers.

By looking at the background of Judas, perhaps one can see why he was the type of person he was. First of all, he was not a Galilean. With the surname, Iscariot, which distinguished him from another Judas who was also an apostle, it indicated that he was from another land, Kerioth. He probably followed Jesus hoping to gain some sort of advantage from the establishment of Christ's kingdom.

Jesus knew his heart but accepted him and trusted him with the moneybag, or treasury, of the twelve. When Jesus visited Mary and Martha of Bethany, Mary used a costly ointment to anoint the feet and hair of Jesus. Judas protested, saying the ointment, worth around three hundred denarii should have been put in his purse and given to the poor. Jesus knew, as is recalled in John 12, that Judas was a thief and wanted the money so he could take some for himself. Judas could have cared less about the poor.

When Jesus mildly reminded Judas of his errors, Judas resented it and went to the Jews and prepared to betray Jesus. For thirty pieces of silver, about $19.50 in U.S. currency, the price of a slave, Judas prepared to sell out his soul. Yet he continued acting dumb about it.

At the Last Supper, Jesus told the disciples, "One of you will betray me." Judas asked, "Is it I lord?" Jesus stated, "You have said so," which meant

"Yes," and told Judas that what he had to do he should do quickly. Judas immediately left the room. He did not partake of the sacrament of the Last Supper.

Later, in the Garden of Gethsemane, chief priests and elders armed with swords and staves came to arrest Jesus. They had prepared Judas to point Him out. Judas walked up to Jesus and saluted Him with a kiss. His dirty work was done. Jesus was seized. The next morning Judas had second thoughts, but it was too late. He realized he had sinned, but no one in authority cared. He went and hanged himself.

In the book of Acts, chapter 1, verse 18, reference is made to this hanging. With the money, Judas evidently bought a field, possibly where he took his life. During the act of hanging, it is written that he fell headlong and his body-busted open in the middle and all of his bowels gushed out. This act of the spilling out of his bowels was part of the punishment for traitors. Here, it happened without another human present.

All the inhabitants of Jerusalem knew what Judas had done. They named the field Judas had purchased, the "Field of Blood," for he bought it with the price of blood. David, in Psalms 109, makes reference to what would happen to Judas. Now the Scriptures were fulfilled once again.

Judas Iscariot could have asked Almighty God for mercy and forgiveness, but he did not. Having not done so, it is evident in Scripture that he is a lost man.

MARY MAGDALENE

There is no doubt that there are people living today possessed by the devil himself. Little attention, if any, is paid to them. Some are put into institutions and locked away. When Jesus walked on this earth, He took care of the matter when He ran across such individuals.

Mary Magdalene was one of them. The Bible records in several places that Jesus did indeed cast seven demons out of this woman. She was a resident of Magdala, or existed in the wretched village of el-Mejdel, about three miles north of Tiberias.

Mary Magdalene was very close to Jesus. When we are grateful to Him who sets us free, we will be close to Him. Such was the case in this woman of ill repute who experienced a changed life.

It is believed to have been Mary Magdalene who anointed the Savior's feet in the city of Galilee (Luke 7:36-50). If this is the same woman, which most scholars believe it was, here is where she receives even more than forgiveness.

At the house of a Pharisee, where Jesus was invited for a meal, arises this woman who is termed "sinful." She had heard that Jesus was visiting there, she arrives uninvited, and begins to wash His feet with expensive ointment. The Pharisee quickly condemns her, informing Jesus she is a sinful woman. But the woman continued washing His feet with her tears and drying them with her hair, certainly a symbol of a repentant soul. She continues by kissing His feet and applying the ointment.

The Pharisees now doubt if Jesus is a prophet saying that if He were, He would have known who she was and wouldn't have allowed this sinful woman to even touch Him.

Jesus knew how to handle people like that and told them a parable. He inquires of them if one man owned you $500 denarii, and the other $50, and neither could pay you back, and you forgave their debt, which one would be the most appreciative? A man called Simon, assumed to be the Pharisee, replies, "The one, I suppose, to whom he forgave more." Jesus replied that he was correct.

Jesus goes on to elaborate His parable. "Look at this woman," he orders them. He informed them that when Jesus came into the Pharisee's house, no one washed His feet or offered water so He could do it Himself. In those times, the feet were the main method of transport. Dirt and dust settled on travelers' tired feet and the custom at the time was to have their feet washed before lodging for the evening. The Pharisee had not given Jesus a kiss or anointed His head with oil, but she did!

Jesus continued, "Though her sins may be many, they are forgiven, for she loved much. But he who is forgiven little, loves little!"

Then those sitting at the table mumbled among themselves inquiring, "Who is this who even forgives sins?" With a look of kindness Jesus looked at Mary and simply stated, "Your faith has saved you, go in peace."

The Pharisees continued to hold it against Jesus that He thought He could forgive sins. They thought Jesus was a blasphemer. They later crucified Him for acts such as this along with other wrongful and untruthful thoughts and rumors they conjured together.

Mary Magdalene was among those who "ministered" to Jesus later in His life. She, among others, supplied whatever they had to help sustain Jesus. They were all sinners, the Pharisees would have said. Without them, Jesus would have been alone. No so-called "righteous" individual, such as a Pharisee, would have let themselves be seen in Jesus' presence.

It was Mary Magdalene who wept at the foot of the cross when Jesus was crucified. It was Mary Magdalene among those who saw to the burial of Jesus and His embalming. Finding the tomb opened, it was this so-called sinful woman who informed the rest of the disciples that Jesus had arose. And finally, it was to this woman to whom Jesus appeared first after He had been resurrected from the grave.

It may be interesting to note that if He would have appeared to one of these so-called "Godly" Pharisees, they would not have believed Him anyway. They later thought someone had stolen the body and believed Christ died but never arose. This misinformation still permeates some of the Jewish community to this day. How sad! If that were the case, that He never arose, we have no hope!

Individuals like Mary Magdalene have hope. They know better. The sinners often know more about Salvation than those who study theology. One cannot pour Jesus into a test tube and try to analyze His purpose. Like Jesus assured Mary Magdalene, "Your faith has saved you!"

THE ACTS

In the book of Acts, reference is made to numerous individuals who followed Jesus and His teachings. Two of those people were a husband and wife by the name of Ananias and Sapphira.

The story is told in Acts 4-5 that a group of believers decided to throw all of their possessions into a pot and follow Christ. If they had money, they put it all in the pot. If they had land or property, they sold it and put it in the same pot. The money was then distributed out to those as needed.

Ananias and Sapphira had sold some property, but knowingly kept a portion of it back, hiding it from the rest. Peter, full of the Holy Spirit, knew what they had done and called Ananias on it. He asked Ananias why he had done such an evil thing. "How is it you have contrived this deed in your heart?" he asked Ananias. Peter continued, "You have not lied to men but to God!"

A very strange thing happened when Peter was finished reprimanding Ananias. Ananias fell dead! About three hours later Ananias' wife, Sapphira, came into the room. Peter started in on her with his reprimand. She, too, fell dead!

What does this story say to us? Does it mean we can't hide things from God? Of course. Does it instill great fear within us, as it did with the early church? I believe we are to conduct ourselves as Jesus told us. *"Render unto Caesar the things that are Caesar's, and to God the things that are God's!"* (Matthew 22:21). What we have belongs to God. What else can we do but return it to Him? Tithing, a Scriptural way of practicing Christian giving, is one

way to return to God what is God's. Who knows
what the consequences will be if we don't.

STEPHEN

I feel it's important to mention Stephen, the first Christian martyr. He was a man who the Bible says was *full of grace and power"* (Acts 6:8). He was so full of these qualifications that he was a threat to the people who were much like those who crucified Christ. They accused him of blaspheming the Holy Scripture. While being accused, it is noted that Stephen "had the face of an angel." His accusers were fearful of him.

In his defense, Stephen delivered a sermon. He recalled stories from the Old Testament. He concluded his message with a stern reprimand to his accusers. Stephen declared that he saw God and Jesus standing on the throne, and the people couldn't take it anymore. They grabbed him, took him out of town and stoned him to death. He proclaimed the Gospel and was the first to die for it. What an honor. Thousands more would find out what a martyr's death would be like. Practically all of the apostles, and many disciples of Jesus, would die for the sake of Jesus Christ.

SAUL, WHO BECAME PAUL

As a free Roman citizen, whose father was a Pharisee, Saul delighted in persecuting the early Christians. When they stoned Stephen, they laid their coats at the feet of Saul who watched the event and went along with it. He continued helping his peers drag Christians out of their homes and off to prison. He boasted that he was going to murder Disciples of Christ.

Often in life, things change. Sometimes a course of events takes place that changes a person. At other times, miracles occur that change lives forever. For Saul, it took a miracle.

On his way to Damascus to find more followers of the Lord and bring them back to Jerusalem for sentencing, a very bright light flashed above him along with a voice, which asked, *"Saul, Saul, why do you persecute me?"* Saul answered, *"Who are you Lord?"* The voice responded, *"I am Jesus, whom you are persecuting, but rise and enter the city, and you will be told what you are to do"* (Acts 9).

Saul arose, but he could not see. He had been struck blind. Those traveling with him could not understand what took place. They, too, had heard the voice but saw no one. His friends led him by the hand into the city of Damascus. For three days, he was blind and refused to eat or drink.

In Damascus, God prepared a man by the name of Ananias who would lay his hands on Saul and restore his sight. When the event took place, objects resembling scales fell off the eyes of Saul, and his sight was restored. At first, Ananias did not want to help this guy who hated Christians. The Lord, through the "voice," convinced him that Saul would

170

be the one who would convert the Gentiles and kings and the children of Israel. The Lord reminded Ananias concerning Saul, "I will show him how much he must suffer for the sake of my name!"

The fantastic part about the story of Saul is this. The Bible declares that *"he is a chosen instrument of mine"* (Acts 9:15). When the Lord has need of us, we become his "instruments." Wow! How great to be chosen by God to be His instrument. I am under the pretense that we are all called to be His instruments. We just need to realize it.

Not many days after Saul's conversion, the Jews plotted to kill him. Since Saul was now a Christian, the Jews couldn't tolerate a man like Saul who had much influence in the community to broadcast the fact that Jesus was indeed, "the Son of God!" Furthermore, the Bible says that Saul was able to "prove that Jesus was the Christ."

Saul traveled around, teaching and preaching with others who were followers of Christ. He managed to keep ahead of those who wanted him dead. Later in the Scripture, we find his name is changed to Paul. It is believed he answered to both names, Paul being the most common. It has crossed my mind that perhaps he may have changed his name to hide from his enemies and further spread the Gospel. I am just speculating, but it could be possible.

Paul went on to preach the Gospel. He performed miracles of healing and used his ability to strike people blind upon occasion. He wrote letters to churches, strengthening and admonishing them. He kept Christians in line. He converted thousands, no doubt. Some of those he tried to convert were people in high places. Some were kings, like King

Agrippa, whom I referred to earlier. In Acts 26:28, Agrippa, in the short time Paul tried to convert him, was almost a Christian. Agrippa felt Paul should be a free man probably because Agrippa believed in what Paul preached.

People like Paul were referred to as *"these men who turned the world upside down"* (Acts 17:6). He, and people like him, did just that. Suffering became common to them. Paul suffered much for the sake of the Gospel. Paul suffered it all: he was in and out of prison, beaten, hungry, thirsty, shipwrecked. The Lord said this would happen. Instead of being the one to inflict pain on the Christians, he became one of those being afflicted.

Even in prison, Paul and his brethren, like Silas, saved souls. On one occasion, God created an earthquake that unlocked the cell gates in the prison. A jailer, greatly concerned he would lose his prisoners, was about to commit suicide. If the prisoners escaped, the jailer would die anyway. Paul quickly assured him that they were all there and accounted for. The jailer had no doubt heard Paul and Silas praying and singing hymns prior to the earthquake. He asked, "What must I do to be saved?" This is a question asked by many yet to this day. Paul answered simply, "Believe in the Lord Jesus, and you will be saved, you and your household!"

Here again we see that when one is brought to Christ, the entire household is saved. Perhaps those members in the house that witness the change in one member, all want that for their lives, too. In this case, that very night the whole family was baptized.

For approximately thirty years, from the time of his conversion, Paul spread the Gospel. He was a missionary, teacher and preacher. He referred to himself as *"the least of the Apostles,"* and became one of the greatest (I Corinthians 15:9). Since he persecuted the Church during the early years of his life, Paul felt he should not be honored with such an esteemed title.

He goes on to say another astounding statement: *"But, by the Grace of God, I AM WHAT I AM!"* (I Corinthians 15:10).

What a man this guy turned out to be. Numerous books have been written about him and his exemplary life. Paul didn't understand himself or his actions at times. He wrote to the Romans in Chapter 7, *"I do not understand my own actions. For I do not do what I want, but I do the very thing I hate."* He would sin and ask himself, why did I do it? I know it's wrong, but I did it anyway. Sound familiar? I would imagine we are all much like Paul – not always understanding why we did, or omitted to do a certain thing, but the Holy Spirit reminds us of the sin. It was frustrating for Paul and it certainly is for us. Paul searches for the answer as to why he acted the way he did. He finds it, stating, "Wretched man that I am! Who will deliver me from this body of death? Thanks be to God through Jesus Christ our Lord! So then, I of myself serve the law of God with my mind, but with my flesh I serve the law of sin."

Charlotte Elliot, in the mid 1850's, was no doubt inspired by Paul when she wrote her wonderful hymn. She was a dance hall girl in London – a beautiful lady. One night, while she was performing, a preacher peered into the dance hall and decided to go in and confront her with the Gospel. When she had completed her routine, the bold preacher walked up and told her about Jesus Christ. The Holy Spirit, through this preacher who walked the streets trying to save souls, had convicted this young lady.

Charlotte went home that night and couldn't sleep. The voice of the preacher kept knocking on the door of her heart. At 2 a.m., she jumped up, went to her desk and began to write. She wrote a song that turned out to be so popular that it is still a favorite in Christian churches today. This song forces people to realize that in spite of our humanism, we can still be one of Christ's flock. The song has brought bitter tears to many a repentant heart, as it did to this dance hall girl when she wrote: Just as I am without one plea. But that Thy blood was shed for me. And that Thou bidst me come to Thee, O Lamb of God, I come, I come.

She wrote six verses to the hymn, each one more astounding than the previous. She knew what was expected of her to receive the Lord Jesus. Nothing! Simply receiving is all that God requires. She wrote, "Just as I am Thou wilt receive. Wilt welcome, pardon, cleanse, relieve. Because Thy promise I believe, O Lamb of God, I come, I come."

Paul came to learn this truth well. I am certain that just before the guillotine slammed down and took off his head, he looked up towards the heavens and said, "O Lamb of God, I come, I come."

What will you do when your last hour is up? We know we can't work our way to heaven. Paul also discovered that truth. Many individuals throughout history have learned that no matter what they have done for Christ, they ask, "Was it enough?" And the answer is always, "NO!" Except by the grace of God, no one has a chance to enter heaven. *"For by grace you have been saved through faith, and this not of doing, it is the gift of God - not because of works, lest any man should boast."* Paul said this to the Ephesians in chapter 2, verse 8. Accept the Gift of God. You will do your good works because as Paul says, you are constrained to do so. When you love God, you cannot help yourself but to do only what is pleasing to Him...the one who made eternal life possible.

THE PRODIGAL SON

When Jesus taught, He often used parables to give His audience something they could relate to. The definition of a parable is simply an earthly saying with a heavenly meaning. There are thirty-nine parables from Jesus in the Bible. His listeners were often astounded when they heard these analogies of life. Parables have been responsible for many people to be converted to the Christian faith.

One of His most famous parables is the one entitled, 'The Prodigal Son.' Prodigal means "lost," as you will see in the story found in Luke 15:11.

Jesus told His listeners about a father who had two sons. They were old enough to begin a life on their own. One of the sons chose to stay with his father while the other chose to leave and go out and have some fun. His father gave him his share of his inheritance, so he chose to enjoy it. He would have ample funds to live as he pleased. He left, much to the disappointment of his father, I'm sure. The Bible says that he went to a far country and engaged himself in "loose living – wine, women and song." He had the spirit of "eat, drink and be merry." The money was soon gone, his friends left him, and he was alone. He should have known this would happen. It seems as long as you have money, you have friends who will help you spend it. When it's gone, so are they. I've personally seen it happen in my neighborhood.

The son was hungry. To make matters worse, a famine struck the land he was in, so no one had extra food, either. He got a job feeding hogs, and the Bible says he would have gladly fed on the husks that the hogs left after they had eaten the corn off the cob. He was very desperate and hungry.

Then Jesus drove the point of the story home. In verse 17, it reads, *"but when he came to himself,"* he was driven to stop and think. "Hey," he said, "back home Dad has all these hired servants and plenty of food. What am I doing here starving to death?" He admitted he was wrong. He made plans to go home and tell his father, "I have sinned against heaven before you. I am no longer worthy to be called your son, treat me as one of your hired servants."

He did as he planned. While he was still off in the distance from his father's house, his father recognized him. His father ran to meet him. His youngest son was home again. The son told him all he had planned – that he was no longer worthy to be called his son. His father kissed the boy and gave his lost son the best robe he had. He ordered his servants to kill the fatted calf so they could all eat and celebrate the return of his lost son. "My son was dead and is alive again. He was lost and is found," his father proclaimed.

Now the elder brother arrived at the scene. Jealousy filled his heart. He stated to his father that he had always been faithful to him, did what he was told and his father never so much as gave him a little goat to celebrate with his friends. No celebration had ever taken place in his honor. He wondered why he played the role of the ideal son and never was rewarded for it while his little brother slept with prostitutes and squandered his inheritance. And it appeared that his dad was glad? It didn't make sense to him.

The father quickly reminded him that all that the father has was his. He shouldn't feel bad: his father would not forget him. He commended the son for being loyal. He informed the elder son that it was fitting that they celebrate simply because, "Your brother was dead, and is alive. He was lost, and is found!"

Jesus makes it very clear in Scripture that there is rejoicing in heaven when a sinner repents. The young son had indeed repented. Jesus often refers to the "lost sheep." He considers us as sheep of His fold. When one is found after it had been lost, there is rejoicing.

The father in the parable is like the Heavenly Father. When one of His children, "sons," goes astray and returns, as in the case of the prodigal, the Father is happy. The lost son is forgiven and receives the very best there is – Eternal life with Him. God does not refer to mass multitudes of people who come to Him. It's usually on an individual basis – singularly, as when "one" sinner repents there is rejoicing in heaven. People are converted to Christ individually. Each and every one of us is as important as the next. No one is better than the other is, as the case of the two brothers shows us. Those who have always been faithful reap the rewards of always enjoying fellowship with Christ. Those who go astray reap the same rewards but know they lost all that important fellowship for a time in their life as the prodigal son did. Oh, what a joy it must have been for the prodigal son to be "Home!" He was in fellowship with the father where he knew he should have never left. It was indeed a joyous moment.

I am reminded of the son who never did return home. It goes back to the time of David concerning his third son, Absalom. He was a fine, handsome-looking boy with long, fine hair of which he was most proud. He was also the favorite son of David, at the time. David was completely unaware that his son, Absalom, was also very ambitious.

When visitors would come to the city to visit David with some concern of theirs, Absalom would go out and greet them first. He was a little politician telling them that if he were judge over them, they would be most comfortable. He would act as if he were humble. If they would begin to bow to him, he would stop them and take their hand graciously and bestow a kiss. He used extreme courtesy hoping to eventually gain them all on his side.

Absalom conjured up a plan to rule Hebron. He informed David, his father and king, that he had to fulfill a vow to serve the Lord in Hebron. David thought that was respectable and let him go, unaware that Absalom was doing nothing more than building up an army to attack Jerusalem and dethrone his father, David.

David soon learned of the scheme. The two armies consisting of father against son soon waged war in a dark forest. David's more experienced fighting men easily conquered the army of Absalom. Absalom, seeing his defeat, tried to escape on his mule. Riding at top speed through the forest with low hanging limbs became a death trap to him. With his long flowing hair flying up and down as he rode, he ducked under a low hanging branch, but his hair didn't make it. It became tangled in the branches. Absalom hung from the tree between heaven and earth as his frightened mule kept on running.

Some of David's soldiers saw it all take place. None wanted to kill the son of David, their king, as he hung desperately by the hair trying to free himself. David's captain, Joab, didn't care if the traitor, Absalom, lived or not. When he learned of Absalom's location, Joab went to him and thrust three darts in his heart, which ended Absalom's life.

When David learned of his son's death, he mourned him. He said, "Oh my son Absalom, I would have died instead of you."

In the case of Absalom, his "measure of sin" was full as the Bible talks about. He could have had a change of heart prior to his ambition of taking over the throne. He could have waited to possibly inherit it. He wanted it right away; God could not let that happen. It was not in God's Divine Plan. Woe to those who go against the plan God has set for them. When we try to change His plan, we suffer consequences.

MARY & MARTHA

Few women are mentioned in the Bible. I have tried to touch on some of those that are. Two thousand years ago, and prior to that, most women were not looked upon as being an authority in much of anything, regretfully. They were, as God told Eve in the Garden of Eden, people whom "men would rule over" (Genesis 3:16). Eve was blamed for causing Adam to sin because Adam didn't have the courage to say, "NO!"

The apostle Paul would not allow women to teach or preach (I Timothy 2:12). I wonder what our churches would be like today if women were forbidden to teach Sunday School. Our children probably would not be taught much. It seems that in most churches the women do almost all of the elementary instruction. The matter continues to be a controversial issue.

In the case of Mary and Martha, who Jesus stopped to visit, the question of what is most important to the Lord arises. When Jesus entered the house, we assume that perhaps Mary asked Jesus some questions because the Bible says He was teaching. Martha, on the other hand, busied herself with preparing a meal for her guests.

Martha became upset with the fact that Mary chose to sit at Jesus' feet and listen to him. Martha had to do all the work, or so she felt. Martha confronted the situation and asked Jesus to order Mary to help her. Martha was surprised at the response of Jesus. "Then God" or in this case, Jesus, told her that it was Mary who made the right decision. Jesus, who loved both Mary and Martha, rebuked Martha and chastened her at the same time. God does that with those whom He loves. Jesus tells her, "You are anxious and troubled about many things." In other words, don't let the cares of this world get in the way of listening to Him.

"One thing is needful," Jesus continues. And that is listening to the word of God. Nothing else matters! Jesus is telling us that while we busy ourselves with all the cares of this world, it means nothing in the kingdom of Christ. Martha may have received the reputation of a gracious hostess, but would that help her when she died? Jesus says, "No!" Sitting at the feet of Jesus and being a zealous disciple meant the most in the end.

When I think of those who often stay home from church because they are having company for the noon meal, I think of Mary and Martha. Or those, when a special church service is being conducted and they don't have time for it, I think of Mary and Martha. We tend to focus on the proverbial "cares of this world" and lose sight of Christ. Jesus reprimands us like He did in the case of Martha. While we busy ourselves with many different things, only what we have done with Christ will last.

LAZARUS

It's important to note the story of Lazarus. We find the story in John 11. He lived in Bethany and was the brother of Mary and Martha. Jesus loved this family and was very close to them.

It was Mary who previously had anointed Jesus with precious ointment and wiped His feet with her hair. She and her sister, Martha, hurried to find Jesus when they learned He and His disciples were on the way to Bethany. They found Him and quickly announced, "Lord, he whom you love is ill!"

Jesus informed the sisters that Lazarus would not die, at least not then. What would happen to Lazarus was to be for the glory of God.

Instead of hurrying to the bedside of his friend, Lazarus, Jesus stayed where He was another two days. He told His disciples He wanted to go to Judea. He had recently been there, and the Jews wanted to stone Him. Why, the disciples asked would He want to go back and risk His life again?

After a couple of days of delay, Jesus informed the disciples it was time to go to Bethany. It was too late. Lazarus had fallen asleep – he had died. The disciples didn't understand Jesus when He informed them that He would go there to "awaken" Lazarus. Sure, that would be easy to do if he was indeed just sleeping.

Then Thomas, the pessimist, decided that all the disciples should go with Him. There will be Jews there, too, who will want to kill Jesus. "Let us also go, that we die with Him," Thomas said. His attitude seemed to be, "What's the use; we are going to die anyway." We may as well go and get it over with. At least they could all die together.

By the time the troop got to Bethany, Lazarus had already been dead four days. Martha, seeing Jesus, was disgusted with Him. She probably raised her voice and literally chewed Him out. "Lord, if you would have been here, my brother would not have died!"

Still wanting the blessing she knows that only Jesus can give, she said, "And even now I know that whatever you ask from God, God will give you. Jesus answered, "Your brother will rise again." Martha responded by saying that she knew that, but that didn't do them any good right then.

Jesus must remind her that, " I am the resurrection and the life!" She acted like she knew that, too.

Mary, in the meantime was back at the house. She was probably in the kitchen busying herself with the preparation of a meal for the mourners. Some Jews were there consoling her. Jesus had not yet entered the village but was at the place that Martha had met Him. Martha had hurried home to inform her sister that she went to find Jesus and hastily reprimanded Him out without thinking. They were both devastated by the absence of Jesus when they needed Him the most.

Thinking Mary was going back to the tomb of Lazarus, the Jews had followed her. No doubt they were surprised to see Jesus. They were ready to document some critical information to help crucify Him later.

Sure enough, Mary stated, "Lord, if you would have been here, our brother would not have died!" She wept and caused Jesus to weep also. He was a compassionate Man and perhaps He was weeping at the doubt that Mary and Martha had. He was known for that. Sometimes when people don't believe you, especially something this important, it makes a person very sad. Such was the case with Jesus. He also saw the Jews muttering amongst themselves, chiming in with Mary and Martha. "Yeah, He can heal a blind man but He couldn't keep Lazarus from dying," they mumbled.

Jesus can fix it! He asks, "Where have you laid him?" referring to Lazarus. When they arrived at the tomb, Jesus said, "Take away the stone." Bear in mind that a body, which has laid in a warm tomb for four days would be starting to reek. Martha reminded Him of that. Jesus reminded her that if she would believe, she would see the glory of God.

He turned to the tomb and ordered Lazarus out of the grave. And there he was. He came out wrapped in grave cloths. He was alive! Jesus ordered those standing by to unbind Lazarus and let him go.

The story of Lazarus and his sisters has an important message. Have you ever asked God for help, and He never showed? I think we all have. I think I have stated in an earlier chapter that God always answers our prayers in one of three ways: yes, no, or not yet!

In the case of Lazarus, Jesus had a mission. He needed to show His audience another miracle He would perform for the glory God. The sisters learned a lesson of patience.

God has a mission for our lives. We call upon Him in times of trouble, as the Bible tells us to do. But we see that Jesus can be a mysterious Guy. One of His best friends was dying, and He didn't show up until it was too late, or so it appeared.

I learned a long time ago that it is not right for us to only remember Jesus when we need Him. How about in those times when things are going smooth. Do we call upon His name then in thanksgiving and praise? Most of us fail. But when times are tough, we are the first to cry, "Oh God, where are you?" We wail and moan, waiting for an answer. Often, we cannot expect an immediate response because God may be trying to teach us something. Maybe He thinks he'll let us sweat it out awhile. It'll teach us a lesson. It did with Mary and Martha.

God is often right on time: right there before something terrible happens and right there before we even know of danger. Then He shows up at just the right moment, keeping us safe from all that would harm us. Then, at other times, he shows up at a time that we feel is too late. A loved one is dying with no hope of healing. Death is inevitable. And we ask, "Where was Jesus?" He could have done something, we think. It may take years to find the answer, but the answer is there. Jesus has His reasons, and you can bet 99% of the time we need to be taught something.

Instead of cursing God and wondering where He is, pray for an answer. It will come to you because He has promised, "I will not leave you alone, I will not forsake you!" You have a Comforter that's guaranteed!

Yes, I know, it's often very difficult to understand. Many times I have witnessed disasters that occur in someone's life. I have seen "unchurched" people go to church and have a relationship with God – certainly a positive blessing. Couples who have lost babies at birth become adoptive parents and become a blessing to a child that was unwanted. That is a positive blessing. Disasters caused by tornadoes, fires and floods have brought families together that otherwise would never have known closeness. That is a positive blessing.

Then there are always those few that when disaster strikes, they leave the church and curse God for the rest of their lives. They die sad and broken. And whose fault is that? Not God's! They may have been put through a test and flunked! They hardened their hearts towards God, and the blessing turned into a curse because they broke off a relationship with Christ. The plan may have been to make a better person out of the individual. It helps to remember Moses, who God hardened like fine steel to prepare him for a greater mission.

What's your mission? Perhaps your mission is only to profess Christ. Are you doing that? Don't pave the road for a terrible event to happen in your life just because God wants to get your attention. Examine yourself. The Bible tells us to do that.

If you are churchless, join a good Bible teaching church. Oh sure, you will find people there whom you wonder about – people who are only "professing Christians." Give them a break, God isn't done with them yet. Remember that Jesus likes to hang around churches. As we see in the story of Lazarus, He delights in raising the dead. He enjoys that, and one day we will see Him raise a multitude of people. Just know you are one of them. In order to have true joy here on earth, you need to know where you will end up when your life is over. Jesus can do that for you. With the raising of Lazarus, we can see our own future. Isn't that great?

THE MATTER OF FAITH

One of the most beautiful things about the Bible is the fact that the most important aspect of the Christian life is one word, FAITH. The Bible teaches that we should have "childlike faith." The Bible goes so far as to even define the word, faith. In the eleventh chapter of Hebrews, the author not only defines the word, but also gives examples of all those individuals who lived by faith. Most of them I have talked about in previous chapters.

I believe that with the above truth in mind, God truly did intend us to know what faith is. Here it is: *"Now faith is the assurance of things hoped for, the conviction of things not seen"* (Hebrews 11:1 RSV). It goes on to say that through this little word, faith, we receive Divine approval. By faith, we understand that the world was created by the word of God. God spoke, "Let there be light," and it was there, plain and simple.

Scientists try to analyze the creation of the world and can't seem to prove it. They have theories, of which many well-known scientists now agree, "Are too shallow."

In verse 6, it reads, *"For without faith, it is impossible to please Him!"* What would have happened if Noah would not have believed God? The world would have been destroyed, and you and I wouldn't be here. *"By faith Noah, being warned by God concerning events as yet unseen, took heed and constructed an ark"* the Bible says in verse 7. He believed what God had said. End of story.

By faith, Abraham obeyed when he was called to go to a place God would show him. He went, not knowing where he was going. How many of us would have done that? Most of us think we have to know where we are going before we even think of leaving. Would we have had enough faith if God were to tell us to leave our home and go to a land that He would show us?

Hebrews 11 continues talking about Isaac, Moses, Rahab, Gideon, Samson, David and more that were shining examples of people who lived by faith alone. It was faith that helped them conquer kingdoms, receive promises, close the mouths of lions, escape the sword and go even so far as being able to resurrect the dead. Some were tortured and died a martyr's death, all because of their faith.

Then the Bible makes an interesting comment about these great individuals of faith. They were people "of whom the world was not worthy." They were good people, and the world didn't appreciate them. I believe we have prophets and evangelists today whom, perhaps, the world does not deserve. They are appreciated anyway. The world did not deserve such blessings then, nor does it now.

I have heard it said that when evil triumphs, good men do nothing. I believe that is the case today. We are living in a time when evil is all around us. In some cases the world is going backward instead of forward. When many state legislatures legalize carrying a concealed weapon just so one can defend himself, we have gone downhill. We have backed up at least 125 years. Why?

Many believe it is the fault of the court system. There are too many lawyers that make a living getting people off the hook. Yet our prisons are full, and as one sheriff told me recently, the county supervisors instructed him to not even pursue a case if he knew that case would end up in court. The county simply did not have the funds to prosecute the case nor to keep someone in jail. What is going on here? It's like having no law at all, and we are living in a lawless society.

Some believe the churches have dropped the ball. When crime seems to be out of control, they blame the churches. Perhaps there is some truth in that. Pastors, unlike those who preached in the last century, tend to preach to the people what the people want to hear. Others say many preachers today fail to present a hunger for the Word in their sermons. People need to hunger and thirst after the Gospel, the Bible says. People need to have the Spirit of God in their lives. There are those pastors who talk a lot about prayer, perhaps, and fail to create a parish who prays. Too often, church members never seem to attach themselves to God. Nothing will happen, for example, if you simply talk about prayer. One must attach themselves to God in prayer before anything can happen.

One of my favorite Scripture verses is Romans 12:2. *"Do not be conformed to this world but be transformed by the renewal of your mind that you may prove what is the will of God, what is good and acceptable and perfect."*

We need our minds renewed! What do we think about? What are our priorities in life? What are we going to do with Jesus? Someone once said that each and every one of us is the prophet of our own life. What we do, what we say, how we think and how we conduct ourselves will determine whom we are serving. Will it be Christ or the world, is the questions each and every one of us must ask ourselves.

Most people who belong to a church give God an opportunity to work in their lives. If you aren't a faithful member of a good Bible teaching church, I would urge you to find one. THEN GOD can work in your life!

BIOGRAPHY

The author is a native of Upland, living south of town on a farm where he was born and raised. He has had an interest in farming most of his life.

In 1973, upon the passing of his father, Edward, a well known Biblical scholar in the area, Ivan began his ministry picking up the proverbial "mantle" left lying vacant by his father.

Ivan has taught Sunday School, Bible classes and has been a lay preacher for nearly thirty years and to answer the many questions given to him, he has been prompted to live the way his father did - by the admonishment in the Bible which tells us to "Search the Scriptures," the inspired word of God Himself to receive the answers.

The love of God and country has stimulated Ivan into writing. He wrote his first book, **"Whiteout 96,"** which is a book about the blizzard on January 17, 1996 which paralyzed the area and trapped many people while traveling.

Because of his interest in people and how they respond during a crisis, he is writing a new book, **"Operation Recognition,"** which focuses on the many military veterans of Nebraska and their stories of fighting for our nation's freedom and why that's important to us.

Ivan is a member of the Nebraska Writer's Guild, Lion's Club and a columnist for a daily newspaper.

"Then God," was written with sinners in mind. You will clearly see in this book how God changes things. When we sin, **"Then God,"** turns us and the situation around making something great and beautiful out of what was a bad situation. He performed such moving acts without obscurity, which is documented in Scripture. These acts indicate that God is not done with us and there is indeed hope.